GOD'S CHURCH
HENRY FLAGLER'S LEGACY

GOD'S CHURCH
HENRY FLAGLER'S LEGACY

The Royal Poinciana
Chapel

ONE HUNDRED YEARS
a history by SANDRA THOMPSON

To the memory of Henry Morrison Flagler
and to all who enter The Little White Church By The Trail
seeking refuge and solace. . .

The Royal Poinciana Chapel
60 Cocoanut Row
Palm Beach, Florida 33480

COVER DESIGN: SANDRA THOMPSON

Artist Frank Beatty attended the Chapel and lived in a modest
apartment in West Palm Beach. Dr. Lindsay commissioned him to
paint the Chapel on two occasions - once in 1965 and again in 1969.
When the painting depicted the tree-shaded Chapel with grey roof,
Dr. Lindsay requested the artist make it more colorful - thus the red
roof. "Dr. Lindsay also had Beatty perform a painting of the white-
roofed manse," according to Marilyn Polete, "and he again requested
that the artist paint the roof and even the front door a bright red."

The painting on the back cover is by Sandra Thompson,
a realist, who would not alter the true color of the Chapel even
if Dr. Lindsay, with persuasive Scottish charm, requested more color.
The painting, contributed by the artist for a fund-raising auction,
was given to Dr. Cromie as a gift.

Published by: Southeastern Printing
                    Stuart, Florida
Design Coordinator: David Basom Jr.

CONTENTS

THE LITTLE WHITE CHURCH BY THE TRAIL   i

PREFACE   ii

INTRODUCTION   v

HENRY MORRISON FLAGLER   1

THE PONCE de LEON   17

EARLY PALM BEACH   25

FLAGLER'S CHURCH   40

DR. GEORGE MORGAN WARD   47

FLAGLER'S PASTOR   63

DR. WILLIAM EDWARD BIEDERWOLF   78

WAR YEARS AND DR. CHARLTON   94

DR. LINDSAY   103

60 COCOANUT ROW   132

DR. MILLER - A BRIDGE BETWEEN   147

RETURN OF SEA GULL AND A NEW MINISTER   173

THOMAS WILLIAM KIRKMAN AND RUTH   180

RENEWAL AND EXPANSION   193

DR. RICHARD MARLIN CROMIE   227

AN ODE TO THE FUTURE   245

THE LITTLE WHITE CHURCH BY THE TRAIL

There's a church that we know as the Chapel
A little white church by the Trail
Way down where the summers are staying
Far away from the snow and the gale.

In the midst of a marvelous city
Where mansions of beauty abound;
It stands for the lowly and holy
With the palms softly waving around.

It points with a modest white steeple
To the blue of the tropical sky
In the hearts of the worshiping people
Its memory never will die.

A lifetime of loving and giving
Christ's message that never will fail;
Is the work of our own dear Chapel
Of the Little White Church by the Trail.

—Amy Albee Newcome

The Ceiba (pentandra) tree has offered shade for over one hundred years to the land that Henry Flagler purchased from the Brelsford family in 1892. The tree stands majestically behind the Chapel and is listed as one of the oldest trees on the island of Palm Beach.

PREFACE

When Hank McCall asked me to write the history of the Royal Poinciana Chapel, I was challenged by the task. While my writings have been primarily biographical, never has the subject been a building.

Hank McCall deserves credit for supplying the vast array of material that fills this work, as a gifted and determined ferreter, spending many hours pulling photographs from the vast collection of the Palm Beach Historical Society as well as reading through Chapel meeting minutes and searching for sermons of yesteryear. His copious harvest resurrected various random short historical pieces and poems and descriptive narratives concerning the various transitions of the venerable Chapel. Hank's abiding enthusiasm is inestimable and wonderfully contagious.

As I began organizing the material and placing the puzzle pieces in appropriate, designated slots, I realized that the Chapel History is not unlike any other memoir, its color and life derived from the people who, over the hundred years since its inception, have entered through the hallowed portals and left their considerable imprints.

Henry Flagler had the original Chapel built in 1897, after completion of the Royal Poinciana Hotel. The Chapel is only one of many facets that comprise the Great Man's legacy — a legacy that enriches not only Palm Beach, but most every community in Florida. While the Empire Builder is credited with the original housing and the precepts that govern it to this day, there have been many individuals who have been instrumental in the furtherance of the Chapel — people who served in the pulpit, those who took chairmanships and served on committees and even those who sat in the sanctuary as members of the congregation. To all, I am indebted for the rich material that was placed before me.

Through the process of writing this history there are many members of the Chapel who were generous, sharing unique and varied perspectives. For their contributions I wish to thank Marjorie Whittemore, James Arnold, Jr., William Tell, Lois Krueger, Hazel Kennedy, Eddie Little, Ted Hepburn, Barbara Pearson Johnson, Margaret Waddell, Donald and Anne Carmichael, Louise Gillett, Judy Golembiewski and George Slaton. I give special thanks to Marilyn Polete whose memory of Dr. Lindsay's years were gained through her devotion to the minister and his wife not only as secretary to the minister but as a surrogate daughter. In addition, Marilyn's ability at the computer is invaluable.

As the work progressed, there was a decision to make; whether to include episodes that were, sadly, uncharacteristic and divisive within the membership to wrench the foundation of Flagler's Church. I felt the inclusion lent credibility to the very existence and survival of not only the Chapel but to those who were determined to see it persevere under extreme adversity.

Early in the writing process, I spoke to Muriel Catuna and Marshall McDonald as well as Dorothy Nixon, the daughter of Carl Eiser - Mr. Eiser was in a nursing home at the time. Sadly, all three voices have been stilled before they could appreciate their inclusion in this written history, but their valuable contributions are substantial and continue to influence the flow of history. However, it is prophetic that through the sad demise of members, the Chapel survives and gives witness to those who have served in the past and survives with a spirit and sense of immortality that quietly pervades the ancient wood sanctuary and beyond.

While there have been many transitory influences determined blessedly by caring guardians, we know not what lies ahead as each minister lends divine prophesy to reach out and serve an ever-increasing needful audience. Hopefully, The Little White Church by the Trail will always remain a source of spiritual enlightenment - a beacon, shining brightly, for all who wish to worship there.

I wish to extend appreciation to Harold F. Powell, Ph.D. for scholarly editing and critique of this treatise commemorating the good work that Henry Flagler initiated years ago. Also special acknowledgment to Jessica Johnston, Public Affairs Director, The Flagler Museum, for photographs and pertinent detail regarding the Flagler era. And it is with a great deal of gratitude that I thank the University of Georgia Press for permission to use Sidney Walter Martin's FLORIDA'S FLAGLER* as a major source pertaining to Henry Morrison Flagler.

It is a distinct privilege for me to be a part of this history, this extraordinary memoir. And I know that it is but one of many histories, a compendium, another piece of a puzzle far from completion. As time passes, there will be much to add in a continuous wedding of people and a simple white Meeting House that Henry Morrison Flagler provided to serve his GOD and humankind.

Sandra Thompson

*reprinted in 1998 under the title
Henry Flagler; Visionary of the Gilded Age

$\mathscr{I}$NTRODUCTION

The Royal Poinciana Chapel history would not be complete without the inclusion of a chapter chronicling the early life of Henry Morrison Flagler. To understand the passage and the many significant influences on the young man is to more fully appreciate the very existence of the Chapel, particularly since his early years and associations are quite disparate from the land developer, builder of railroads and pioneer adventurer who transformed the tropics. His is a fascinating progression after leaving the security of family at fourteen and the opportunity for formal education to become immersed in the corporate world where unparalleled opportunities brought riches far beyond anyone's imaginings. It was, then, prophetic that Henry Flagler discovered Florida and used his magnificent business sense and enormous wealth to establish, among many other wonderful contributions and amenities, the humble Chapel where today, like in days of old, family and friends gather, listening to Godly words that offer answers to life's trials, words to inspire renewal and hope.

The Chapel history, reflected in the antique glass of the sanctuary windows, just as the simple white building of the late eighteen hundreds, is a symbol separate from and yet a part of its environment. Palm Beach has changed dramatically over the years, but the Chapel has remained steadfast in an atmosphere where wealth and societal mores are diametrically opposite from the utter simplicity of the edifice and the message emanating from its pulpit.

Fortunately little has changed of the original, unadorned Chapel, but let us step back in time to when it was quite different, when it all began for Henry Morrison Flagler, for Palm Beach and for the very special Royal Poinciana Chapel.

Henry Flagler - Young Businessman

$\mathcal{H}$ENRY MORRISON FLAGLER

It was cold in January of 1830 when Henry Morrison Flagler was born and perhaps cold in October, fourteen years later, when he began his long journey from Hopewell, in upper New York State, a journey that would ultimately lead to the tropical jungle of south Florida. One could hardly consider a more dichotomous scenario so very far from any imaginings of the young man leaving the warm shelter of a modest home — one in which loving parents and an adored sister provided the only security he had ever known. Henry was driven by the knowledge that jobs were scarce and his father, an itinerant Presbyterian minister, could barely afford to provide for his family. Henry sought to carve an independent living. Little did he know then that his path would take him to a paradise so very far away not only from Hopewell but from every ancestral habitat both foreign and domestic.

The young man leaving formal education after completing the eighth grade could trace his ancestry to Zacharra Flegler, a carpenter, who immigrated to America in the early eighteenth century from Franconia via England. Zacharra settled along with other Franconians, after arriving in New York, in small settlements along the banks of the Hudson, some in Columbia County and others in Ulster and Dutchess Counties.

To Zacharra Flegler were born three sons, Philip Solomon, Simon and Zachariah. Zachariah, like his father, married three times and to his wives were born sixteen children. Solomon Flegler was the eighth child, born in 1760, the grandfather of Henry Morrison Flagler and it was Solomon who changed the spelling of the name from Flegler to Flagler. Solomon fathered eleven children, the fifth, Isaac, born 1789, was father to Henry Morrison Flagler.

Isaac grew up in Pleasant Valley with little formal education although he was widely read. Ordained a Presbyterian minister, after losing his first wife, he accepted a call to be minister in Milton, New York, where he married his second wife who gave birth to a daughter, named Carrie. When his wife died after three years of marriage, he was left a widower with a young daughter and soon met a widow named Elizabeth Caldwell Harkness. Elizabeth had been married twice, first to Hugh Morrison of Washington County New York, and then to David Harkness, a physician from Bellevue, Ohio, with whom she had a son named Daniel M. Harkness. It was in Salem, New York, where Elizabeth met Isaac Flagler soon after the death of her second husband. Isaac was serving a pastorate in Seneca County, New York at the time.

Shortly after the marriage of Isaac to Elizabeth, they moved to Hopewell, where Henry Morrison Flagler was born January 2, 1830. Named for an uncle, Henry Flagler, and Elizabeth's first husband, Hugh Morrison, Henry was fourteen when he decided that neither the ministry nor farming were callings for him. He was tempted to leave Hopewell in response to glowing reports from half-brother Daniel, promoting opportunities for employment with the family company, L.G. Harkness & Company, in Republic, Ohio.

Henry completed eighth grade before dropping out of school. He worked for a time as a deck hand on a canal boat out of Medina, New York. When he decided to join Daniel in Ohio and had the blessing of his parents, he began the long trek, walking the first nine miles into Medina where he lingered long enough to plan the ongoing journey - first by boat some fifty miles through the Erie Canal to Buffalo and then on to Sandusky, Ohio on the southern shore of Lake Erie, a crossing that took three days and nights. After a rough passage it took several days to recover before the final progression, probably on foot, thirty miles to Republic, a small town populated by less than a thousand.

Henry arrived in Republic with less than a dime in his pockets. He was met by half-brother Dan and went to work immediately at the General Store learning sales and merchandising. His salary of five dollars per month included room and board — which was a shared room with Dan behind the store. The crude accommodation was not properly heated and often the young men slept beneath a counter in the store, huddled together for warmth. Young Henry was learning survival tactics. It was 1844 and Henry's potential fortune was impossible to conjure — it was not even a pipe dream for the young lad to indulge.

The new employee was anxious to please and wanted badly to impress not only half-brother Dan but also Lamon Harkness, Dan's uncle who ran the business. Henry worked long hours six days per week proving himself an invaluable employee. By necessity he learned to be frugal and prudent and was soon acknowledged as a teenage businessman and taken in as a partner in Harkness & Company. When the firms were reorganized and named Chapman, Harkness & Company, Henry took Dan's place as manager of the Republic store. His salary in 1849 jumped to four hundred dollars per year when he moved to the store in Bellevue, where the population was growing and business was booming. He also became witness to fortunes building.

It was in 1839, before Henry arrived on the scene, when the railroad came to Bellevue. In view of the potential population explosion, business associates F. A. Chapman, T. F. Amsden and L. G. Harkness bought most of the town's property. Ten years later, Henry watched the sale of much of the properties to newcomers for highly escalated prices. The men became the wealthiest and most influential citizens of Bellevue. Henry Flagler was learning well how wealth and power were acquired.

Most of Henry's after-work hours were spent with the Harkness family. Henry ultimately married Mary, daughter of Lamon Harkness, on November 9, 1853. It was a happy union from the start.

When the company expanded into the distillery and grain and liquor business, their volume doubled and Flagler's salary was enhanced dramatically by commissions. Henry was in a position to buy Chapman's interest in the company when the senior partner retired. The business was engaged in shipping large quantities of wheat to market in Cleveland, where a man named John D. Rockefeller, a commission merchant, handled most of the shipments coming from the newly incorporated Harkness and Company. The two young businessmen met at that time but little did they know what the future held. However, each was goal oriented with their sights on financial success, never realizing that the measure of that success would be jointly achieved and of enormous proportions. It is of note that in Cleveland, John D. Rockefeller would become well acquainted with a young Scottish gentleman named Sam Lindsay who became his golfing partner — but that comes later.

Mary and Henry Flagler, happily married, were busy raising their family in Bellevue until 1862. However, there was sadness and tragedy as well. Business was good but the political climate was disturbing. The argument between the North and South over extension of slavery was polarizing the nation.

The marriage was blessed by the birth of a daughter, Jenny Louise, in March of 1855. Another daughter, Carrie, was born in 1858 and Henry's life revolved around business and family and church. Since there was no Presbyterian Church in Bellevue, they were members of the Congregational Church. When frail little Carrie died at three years of age, it seemed a cruel blow to Henry and was almost more than Mary, never a robust woman, could abide. Their religious faith sustained the young parents.

Flagler, a Republican, most likely disagreed with the decision in the Dred Scott case in 1857 and no doubt cheered Lincoln's rise to prominence just prior to the election of 1860. He was aware of the significance of the Republican victory and was not surprised when the southern states began to secede from the Union.

Lincoln's call for volunteers was answered by many. Dan Harkness was one of the first to offer his services to the Union Army. Henry felt war was wasteful and that a compromise was far better for the nation. However, he hired a substitute to serve for him, paying three hundred dollars in what was a legal arrangement at the time. John D. Rockefeller, it is noted, was another who did not enlist but chose to remain actively engaged in commerce during the war.

The military conflict increased the volume of grain business many times over. The war went on for four years and the industry, in support of the war effort, created a prosperous atmosphere for the businessmen. However, there was sadness and personal loss for Henry. Mary's delicate health was a concern and in 1861 Henry lost his beloved mother, Elizabeth. His father, Isaac, would survive his wife by many years.

It was 1862 when Henry had accumulated $50,000 and sought another business opportunity to accumulate money faster. He was willing to gamble on a new, exciting endeavor — the salt business. His father-in-law, L. G. Harkness, had taken the leap. Henry watched as L. G. bought shares in the East Saginaw Manufacturing Company. Henry finally yielded to temptation and in 1862 cast his fortune with the new industry, pulling up stakes in Bellevue and moving his family to Saginaw, Michigan. His investment seemed secure enough and the Flaglers became entrenched in Saginaw, joining the Congregational Church, just recently united with the Presbyterian Church. Flagler was made superintendent of the Sunday School and member of the board of trustees. All was well as an equal partner in the firm of Flagler & York. His partner, Barney York, was a brother-in-law who borrowed money from his father-in-law to enter into the highly competitive business venture. Unfortunately, the newly formed partnership did not dominate the market as other salt-producing companies were formed in Saginaw.

Making good salt was not so easy and when the price of the hot commodity collapsed at the close of the war, Flagler was left with nothing. Salt was used to cure food. When the war ended the need diminished dramatically. By late 1865 he'd lost everything and was a wounded warrior, humiliated by the financial failure, in such strong contrast to the success that he had achieved so quickly early in his career. He could have returned to Bellevue and the grain business there, but he chose to go to Cleveland, a city on the rise and one that seemed to offer the best opportunity to pay off his debt — money borrowed from father-in-law, Dan Harkness. Henry was embarrassed by the need and determined never to be poor again — he abhorred owing money to anyone.

Cleveland was a robust town located on the southern shores of Lake Erie and blessed with unrivaled transportation facilities — served by five railroads. With only a few hundred dollars in his pocket Henry set up a grain business after moving his family into modest quarters. To supplement the meager funds he tried making barrels and even went into the business of marketing special horseshoes. The grain business did not prosper and Flagler became despondent. When he met Maurice B. Clark, a grain commission merchant associated with John D. Rockefeller, an offer was forthcoming that would prove prophetic for the businessman.

Rockefeller was abandoning the grain business to go into the oil business. Clark invited Flagler to become a partner with him in the grain company, Clark & Sanford. While Rockefeller went to the oil industry, he remained in Cleveland and a friendship developed between he and Flagler.

Petroleum, an untapped resource before 1800, became a vital industry in Pennsylvania, Kentucky and Ohio, with traces found by speculators drilling for salt. Used initially for medicinal purposes and also as a fuel for illumination in business and factories, the demand rapidly increased. As oil became the treasured natural resource, oil men and others associated with the industry made a great deal of money.

Henry Morrison Flagler 1830-1913

FLAGLER MUSEUM ARCHIVES

Cleveland soon became the hub, with oil being shipped to the port city for refinement and then on to other cities. When Rockefeller sought expansion capital for his oil business, he went to Steven V. Harkness and an agreement was struck stipulating that Harkness would contribute the capital as long as Henry Flagler was to have control of the investment. Rockefeller now had a brilliant businessman in allegiance in a partnership of Rockefeller, Andrews and Flagler — the beginning of a petroleum oligarchy.

With offices in Cleveland and New York City, the organization was soon heralded as the oldest refining business and one of the largest in the United States. The association would last for a decade and the friendship between Flagler and Rockefeller grew stronger. They both lived in fine homes on Euclid Avenue, considered to be one of the most prestigious avenues in any American city.

On March 5, 1867, the new firm advertised its product in the *Cleveland Leader*, announcing its offices in Cleveland at the Case Building, and in New York at 181 Pearl Street. The *Leader* article commented on the new partnership:

> "Our readers will notice by the advertisement in another column, that the old and reliable firm of Rockefeller and Andrews has undergone a change, and now appears under the new title of Rockefeller, Andrews, and Flagler. This firm is one of the oldest in the refining business and their trade, already a mammoth one, is still further enlarged by the recent change: so that with their New York house, their establishment is one of the largest in the United States. Among the many oil refining enterprises, this seems to be one of the most successful; its heavy capital and consummate management, having kept it clear of the many shoals upon which oil refining houses have so often stranded."

In 1870 Mary gave birth to a son. Flagler was now the proud parent of Harry Harkness Flagler. While business was compelling, even when the business expanded to overseas markets and Flagler and Rockefeller were ecstatic, there was also continuing strife and tragedy in Flagler's life. Due to Mary's poor health their social activities were limited. It was said that for the last seventeen years of Mary's life, from 1864 to 1881, Flagler spent only two evenings away from home. In spite of a multiplicity of commitments he found time to take the children on picnics and he involved himself as an active participant in the life of the city. He was a member of the Cleveland Board of Trade and the Manufacturers Association of Cleveland. Two years after the Civil War ended, he urged the Board of Trade to donate money for the destitute people of the south where the ravages of war had taken a tremendous toll.

Flagler's business responsibilities included dealing with railroads in freight-rate negotiations. Flagler initiated rebates which gave the firm great concessions propelling them into favorite status as refiners. Flagler began seeking smaller refineries to buy out and his resultant success was the precursor to Standard Oil Company. Its partners in the company incorporating in 1870 were: John D. Rockefeller, Henry M. Flagler, Samuel Andrews, Stephen V. Harkness and William Rockefeller, with capital reported at one million dollars. When Rockefeller was asked if the incorporated company was the result of his planning he answered, "No, sir, I wish I'd had the brains to think of it. It was Henry M. Flagler." The oil giant was soon producing one-tenth of all the petroleum business in the United States. As the plan to buy out any and all competitors was put in place the reputation for 'freezing out' others created a great antipathy toward the two principal partners of Standard Oil. By 1878 Standard Oil controlled most of the pipelines carrying petroleum from the oil-rich regions, thereby gaining the position to dictate rates received from the railroads. It was the same year that Flagler studied law and in two hundred words drafted the charter for the Standard Oil Corporation.

In the late 1870s the family still maintained their home in Cleveland but visited New York and took accommodations at a hotel while in the eastern city. When Mary's bronchial condition worsened, on doctor's orders, they decided to spend part of the winter in Florida. Florida at the time was primarily marshlands and mangrove with few human inhabitants and a great deal of wildlife, unmolested by man other than Indians and early settlers. Jacksonville was the southernmost area of population accessible at that time by rail. However, Flagler was disappointed in the lack of proper hotel or transportation facilities in a portion of the country reputed to offer such wonderful therapeutic qualities to the elderly and infirm.

While Mary rested well in Jacksonville, Flagler could not remain in Florida for more than a few weeks and she did not care to stay in Florida with the children unaided by her husband. They changed their New York residence to another hotel before Flagler purchased a house on the corner of Fifty-fourth Street and Fifth

Avenue. When Mary's lung problems prevented further travel, Henry realized that even the Florida sunshine could not make her better. On May 18, 1881 Mary Harkness Flagler died. Her death had a profound effect on Henry, leaving him, sadly, to care for young Harry, only eleven at the time. Henry rented a large house at Mamaroneck on Long Island Sound, with thirty-two acres surrounded by water. When he purchased the property, called Satanstoe, he paid $125,000 which was a considerable amount of money back then; he called the magnificent estate Lawn Beach and spent nearly a quarter million dollars improving it.

Flagler attempted to overcome the grief he felt in losing his beloved wife, staying busy with family and a business that, while producing enormous wealth, was also producing enormous stress. His sad demeanor was quite evident to those around him during an extremely difficult time for the wealthy industrialist. While the years between 1870 and 1882 produced the greatest development and growth for the company, its capital increasing to fifty-five million, there was a price to pay. As one after another refining company became allied as affiliates of Standard Oil, the giant became a powerful monopoly governing major railroads and pipelines. This at a time when unification was on the rise in the economic world. There was the realization that more could be accomplished with a bigger, stronger organization. However, there were many victims of the expansion as well as allies. While individuals were hurt, many became wealthy.

At a time of great complexity in business, Flagler remarried. Ida Alice Shourds had been a practical nurse attending Mary Harkness Flagler for years in the Flagler home. The marriage took place at the Madison Avenue Methodist Church in New York City on June 5, 1883. Eighteen years younger than Henry, Alice had been raised by her mother, having lost her father, an Episcopal minister, when she was very young. The beautiful red-headed, blue-eyed petite bride had limited formal education and before becoming a practical nurse aspired to being an actress. The union was not entirely pleasing to either the Flagler or the Harkness families. Ida Alice was thirty-five, Henry was fifty-three years of age at the time, and her arrival at the family home was less than welcoming although Henry seemed to genuinely love his new wife and obviously denied her nothing. She was greatly impressed by his wealth and while she tried to be mother to step-son Harry, she was never accepted by the young man as anyone but his father's wife.

Against the background of a new marriage and renewed personal happiness, Flagler was paying a price. In 1879 the combined companies that comprised Standard Oil Company had become known as The Standard Alliance, controlling ninety-five percent of the petroleum industry in the entire country. As Standard Oil's legal mind, Flagler helped determine the form of the modern industrial corporation by establishing the business trust, making it possible, in essence, to establish a multi-state corporation, something entirely new in business. Flagler was listed as secretary and company "lawyer." The new organization brought under one umbrella all the existing stockholders in the various allied enterprises. With over fifty million in capital and properties valued at seventy-five million, the trust was the biggest business in America and its power and stature created growing distrust toward the "monstrous organization." The media only served to exacerbate the building criticism within the industry and Flagler was called to Washington to testify before a United States Senate Committee on many occasions. Through inquiries Flagler revealed that he held a vested interest in three railroads, one of which was the Jacksonville, St. Augustine, and Halifax River Railroad, as well as the Tampa, Jacksonville and Key West Railway. A direct outcome of the investigations of Standard Oil and other monopolies, was passage of the Sherman Anti-Trust Act ultimately passed into legislation in 1890. Vigorous action by the United States Supreme Court resulted in dissolution of Standard Oil Trust in March of 1892 when Flagler, still listed in name only as secretary, had retired from the business. But that's getting ahead of our story.

The belated honeymoon for the newlyweds in December of 1883 allowed the Flaglers to escape the cold winter of New York. Flagler had been to Jacksonville with Mary many times. He was worth close to twenty million dollars and ready to retire. The leisurely trip would be gained by rail, taking ninety hours due to many changes of train on the different gauges of track en route. There was no easy way to journey overland to Florida in those days. One traveller expressed the difficulties:

> "There are two ways of getting to Jacksonville (from Savannah), and whichever you choose you will be sorry that you had not taken the other. There is the night train by railroad, which brings you to Jacksonville in about sixteen hours; and there is the steamboat line, which goes inland nearly all the way, and which may land you in a day, or you may run aground, and remain on board for a week."

A trip to St. Augustine via the St. Johns River proved prophetic. While the Flaglers were less than impressed by the small settlement, they appreciated the climate. The temperature was reported to be minus twenty-seven in some northern cities. They were impressed by the warmth, the abundant orange groves and the flowering beauty of the lush tropics, although St. Augustine, population 2,000, was rundown and lacked development with no large hotel to accommodate the sophisticated Yankees. However, the trip convinced Flagler that St. Augustine had the potential as a resort town, but he wondered why it did not have better facilities for winter visitors.

Due to lack of accessibility, Florida had remained untapped and mostly unpopulated. In 1877 there had been some interest in the region around Daytona and during the winter months stagecoaches had been operating between a place called Enterprise on the St. Johns River and New Smyrna on the coast. In the eighties Melbourne was a small settlement and around the shores of Biscayne Bay there were a few inhabitants. Dade County, which at that time extended from St. Lucie River to Key West, had a population of only 257. Life up and down the Florida east coast was simple with no luxuries or amenities. Settlers fished or hunted and lived off the land. Livestock was almost non-existent. There was an early railroad, a short line of 23 miles from Tallahassee to St. Marks, built in 1834. Other lines were on the drawing boards when the Seminole Indian War in 1836 put an end to most ventures in the state.

Prior to the Civil War there were 416 miles of rail lines, increasing to 485 during the war. However, rail mileage grew rapidly in the early eighties, particularly in East Florida, and the improved transportation served to attract industry and agriculture to what was dubbed "the new South."

In February of 1885 the Flaglers traveled to Jacksonville by private railway car purchased the year before. They again went to St. Augustine via the Jacksonville, St. Augustine & Halifax River Railway. They stayed at the new San Marco Hotel and were duly impressed by the grand hotel and its manager, New Englander Osborn D. Seavey. The newly developing St. Augustine caught Flagler's attention. There was much to be admired not only in better access but in a modern hotel and other new construction, particularly the Villa Zorayda, residence of Franklin W. Smith. Smith, a man who had become interested in building another resort hotel in the city, built his home of a new material made from cement, shells and water. It was an exquisite residence, an exact miniature reproduction of the palace of the Alhambra. The house, square in shape with a courtyard in the center overlooked by balconies, was further enhanced by gardens illuminated at night by colored lamps. The pretentious casa was in sharp contrast to the humble abodes of the past.

At the same time, financier William Astor was building a new rail line from Tocoi Junction just west of St. Augustine to East Palatka. There were other lines being constructed that eventually ran from the St. Johns River to Ormond and Daytona. However, construction was slowed due to marshlands to be filled and the need to cut through coquina rock, done by hand for lack of stone-cutting machinery — all tedious and labor-intensive.

Flagler had been through much in his business career. His enormous wealth, derived from an industry that had come under scrutiny by the United States Government, also received bad press lambasting the 'Robber Barons' for burying the small independent oil refineries and other allied businesses. There had been much in the past, both in business and his personal life, that had been unpleasant. His friends said that he had always wanted to own a hotel, saying that he had been fascinated by the duties of hotel manager. It is incongruous to think that the industrialist would deem to settle for such a mundane position, not to diminish the importance of such labor. But the idea of building a hotel, a positive pleasure-giving activity, must have been appealing and a complete departure from anything that had previously occupied the beleaguered industrialist. Thoughts of building a grand hotel seemed ever closer to becoming reality.

It was March of 1885 when there was a grand celebration in St. Augustine, an elaborate party commemorating the historical landing of Ponce de Leon. The name Ponce de Leon kept playing in Flagler's mind. His hotel would be named the Ponce de Leon! His acquaintance with Andrew Anderson, a prominent citizen of the city and practicing physician born in St. Augustine in 1839, would influence Flagler's ultimate decision. Dr. Anderson, educated at Princeton and the College of Physicians and Surgeons in New York City, owned considerable real estate in St. Augustine and Flagler bought several acres from the good doctor on which to build a magnificent hotel.

In May of 1885 Flagler returned from New York with business associate Benjamin Brewster, known for his ability to evaluate men, property and materials, and Thomas Hastings, a young promising architect who had studied at the prestigious Ecole des Beaux-Arts in Paris. News of Flagler's plans for his first real estate development in Florida spread like wildfire and excited land speculators contacted Flagler with all sorts of proposals. Flagler was focused on what he worked out in the parlor of Dr. Anderson's home — rough sketches of Spanish architecture which ultimately led to blueprints for the Hotel Ponce de Leon. Flagler returned to Mamaroneck leaving Dr. Anderson as his Florida agent and one who had a vested interest in seeing the city of St. Augustine grow. One of Anderson's assignments was to secure permission from the government to quarry coquina from the region. Flagler also wanted the small railroad depot at the San Marco Hotel moved to a central location to better serve both hotels. Henry Flagler promised to donate the land for the depot.

Work began preparing the land for the hotel with obstacles to overcome, one being to fill portions where a creek ran across. There were some disputed land titles to clear but the oil magnate was accustomed to solving problems and clearing monumental obstacles. With Dr. Anderson's help, Flagler persevered.

Before actual building commenced, Flagler invited Dr. Anderson to spend two weeks in Mamaroneck to discuss the project. There were ocean trips on Flagler's yacht, the Columbia, and time for the two men to become better acquainted. Dr. Anderson was greatly impressed by the splendor and wealth of Flagler's northern abode and questioned his interest in "a musty old place like St. Augustine?" Flagler's response indicated that he was willing to gamble on Florida not wholly as a commercial enterprise but largely as a pleasure-giving challenge and activity — to see if he could create in the quaint old town something that would indeed be a successful investment. Flagler, never far from his religious impulses and influence related a story: "There was once a good old church member who had always lived a correct life until well advanced in years. One day when very old he went on a drunken spree. While in this state he met his good pastor, to whom, being soundly upbraided for his condition, he replied, 'I've been giving all my days to the Lord hitherto, and now I'm taking one for myself.'

This is somewhat my case. For about fourteen or fifteen years, I have devoted my time exclusively to business, and now I am pleasing myself." After listening to Flagler's story his companion answered, jokingly, "You have been looking for a place in which to make a fool of yourself, and you've finally chosen St. Augustine as the place."

In fairness, Henry Flagler was a religious man imbued with a firm belief in a personal Deity. It was Dr. Anderson's belief that Flagler felt obligated to use his wealth to create opportunities for others to help themselves. After years of strife in the oil industry, albeit financially lucrative, perhaps his reason for committing such a 'Folly' in the hot, moist tropical wasteland, was more deeply rooted in his reply, "I'm doing it for pleasure." Could there not also be guilt involved in the methods used in acquiring his fortune? It was time to pay back, but more than anything, the challenges were enormous and Flagler must have felt the crest of a tremendous ground swell.

Hotel Ponce de Leon, St. Augustine, completed 1887

$\mathcal{T}$HE PONCE
de LEON

The Ponce de Leon was one of the largest poured concrete structures ever erected on the North American continent. When completed the four storied hotel of coquina gravel mixed with cement,
the magnificent carved and dressed oak interior prepared in New
York, the medieval towers overlooking the Atlantic Ocean, the
sunny courtyards and cool retreats, fountains and towers, combined to take one back to the Spanish Renaissance. The grounds
were beautifully arranged with tropical gardens, overhanging palms
and native shrubbery, the front entrance graced with verandas running along the street on each side of the main gate. Inside the front
gate was an interior court surrounded by vine-bedecked verandas
overlooking a multi-colored fountain planted in exotic evergreens.
Across from the main entrance visitors entered a rotunda through

a grand archway with smaller arches supported by pillars of terra cotta. There was inlaid richly colored mosaic work and a great dome supported by pillars of massive oak.

The old Spanish theme was carried throughout with figures and ornaments using allegorical representations of the elements, fire, water, air and earth. Paintings adorning the interior depicted the Landing of Columbus, the Conquest of Charlemagne and the Introduction of Christianity. Upon entering the dining hall, one was impressed with the stained glass windows designed by Louis Comfort Tiffany, and the magnificent antique oak columns and highly polished floors in an oval-shaped room with seating capacity for seven hundred. The ceilings were designed to depict the sixteenth century history of St. Augustine beginning with the persecutions of the French Huguenots who sought refuge in the New World, and one of Jean Ribaut exploring the coast of Florida in 1562, entering a river which he named the River of May (the St. Johns). There was much that was grand about the Ponce de Leon.

Flagler was determined to have the hotel open for the 1887 season. Delays threatened to extend the hoped for January '88 opening. To hasten the grand opening celebration Flagler was present to help unload schooners arriving in St. Augustine harbor with the hotel furniture aboard. The hotel opened officially January 10, 1888 at a total cost of $2,500,000 and the festivities were indeed grand. Flagler had a prominent New York orchestra travel south to supply the entertainment.

It had been a lengthy process to complete the hotel. There was much to be said in approbation for Flagler's character as a result of his first major independent construction project. Surely much of the attention to detail had to do with the barrage of criticism leveled at the Oil Magnate. It was to be admired that early in the planning stages of the hotel construction Flagler had Dr. Anderson affirm if the St. Augustine board of aldermen had an objection to the project. He also questioned whether digging the foundation might create a malarial epidemic. His concern for the approval of local constituents as well as the health of his workers and the citizens of St. Augustine was commendable.

A story told about Flagler says a great deal for the powerful man who preferred to remain anonymous. He often walked about smoking a cigar. There were "No Smoking" signs placed about the construction site and one day Flagler tried to enter but was stopped by a watchman. The millionaire informed the young man that he was Mr. Flagler, owner of the hotel. The watchman replied, "I can't help that. There have been a good many Flaglers trying to get in here." Flagler later complimented the man on his efficiency.

It wasn't long after the auspicious event, enjoyed by an appreciative audience of visitors from the north, when Flagler realized that he should build a 'sister hotel' catering to those who were not quite wealthy enough to pay the tariff at the opulent Ponce de Leon. The Alcazar Hotel was built across the street. A smaller hotel of Moorish design, in keeping with the Spanish Renaissance styling of the larger hotel, it offered similar amenities. The gardens were lushly planted in tropical flowering shrubbery and trees, surrounding the shops and restaurants and even a gambling casino.

It was in St. Augustine where Flagler became associated with a man named Colonel Edward R. Bradley and the two became partners in the Bacchus Club, a casino in the bustling city. Flagler was anxious for his hotels to offer the very finest facilities and both hotels boasted electric lights which was a novelty to many guests. There were sulphur and salt water pools and so much that appealed to an instant throng of winter visitors. The immediate success of both establishments prompted optimistic thoughts of further expansion and investment in Florida. Another hotel under construction close by was purchased by Flagler and named the Cordova. The Oil Magnate had become a hotelier.

The Flaglers began spending more time in Florida, arriving for the season in their private railroad car, the Alicia. The luxurious accommodation contained several bedrooms, a spacious sitting room, dining room and kitchen. With servants aboard it was an elegant mode of transport. Soon a home was planned to house the family during their lengthy stays in St. Augustine. Called Kirkside, the building was begun in 1892. Located only two blocks from the Ponce de Leon, it was designed for winter living and spacious enough for entertaining. Pure colonial architecture prevailed throughout the fifteen-room structure.

The house, pillared entrance and a salon suggestive of Versailles in all its splendor, provided an ideal setting for lavish parties. Ida Alice enjoyed hosting parties and many were given at the Ponce de Leon as well. Henry Flagler tolerated the social affairs in deference to Ida Alice who was ambitious to be a leading society grande dame although she never quite achieved her goal. However, the parties were elaborate and the Flaglers hosted many dignitaries. One affair was reported by *The Tatler* as the "pearl dance" because of the size and beauty of the pearls Alice wore.

Tragedy and disappointment seemed to go hand in hand with accomplishment and success. When Flagler petitioned his 23 year old son to help run the Florida properties the young man attempted to please his father in an arrangement that lasted for only two years. Young Harry then returned to New York where he became more fully enmeshed in musical circles. Henry Flagler never accepted the rejection and the relationship of father and only son was never close again. The breach was further magnified by the loss of his daughter on March 25, 1889. Jenny Louise had given birth to a baby girl but the child tragically died a few hours after the delivery. Jenny's health was threatened and her physician recommended that she go to Florida. She was in route aboard her father-in-law's yacht, the Oneida, when she became desperately ill and died. She was buried in Woodlawn Cemetery in New York.

Flagler built the First Presbyterian Church in St. Augustine in 1890. The remains of first wife Mary and of Jenny and her infant daughter were moved to a vault adjoining the church. Space for Flagler's tomb was also provided within the mausoleum. Costing $200,000, upon completion, the name was changed to Memorial

Presbyterian Church. Located at the rear of the Ponce de Leon, it was one of the most beautiful adornments of the city, the dome contributing dignity and grace to the skyline. The dedication services in the six hundred seat sanctuary were conducted by eight ministers and an imported choir from New York provided the music. The wife of President Benjamin Harrison attended, along with other distinguished persons.

Flagler's philanthropy knew no boundaries. He helped rebuild the Catholic Church when a fire destroyed most of the Cathedral and when he wished to purchase the property on which the Methodist Church stood, Flagler offered to build a new sanctuary for the Methodists along with a parsonage. He also built a modern hospital in the city which he deeded to a local board of trustees. Anxious to improve 'his city', he contributed to the building of the City Hall and to a Negro school. He was also involved in providing monies for street paving, the establishment of a water works system and electric lights, the laying of sewers and the construction of a number of comfortable homes for his own employees.

Henry Flagler, at age sixty, had begun a new career. He was dynamically and enthusiastically engaged in pioneering and his vision and ambitions would soon take him further south.

During the construction of the Ponce de Leon he became acutely aware that the rickety narrow-gauge railroad from Jacksonville to St. Augustine was inadequate to help build the hotel. He bought the short haul railroad and improved it which only served to facilitate travel possibilities to St. Augustine. Before the Ponce de Leon opened, Flagler had purchased existing short-line railroads and converted them to a standard gauge. His tracks ran along the shore of the St. Johns River in Jacksonville and a bridge to Palatka was also constructed. With the Flagler Florida Empire building, land was purchased and a model farm went in at Hastings where the rural area became noted for potatoes. Acres of orange groves were planted and other farming went in along the rail lines that Flagler owned and soon the railroad and hotel magnate was a farmer, an occupation he rejected in his youth.

To facilitate passengers moving from Jacksonville to St. Augustine, the St. Johns Bridge was constructed, obviating the need for ferrying across the river to south Jacksonville. When the all-steel bridge was completed in 1890 it was one of the finest ever built in the south and would remain in use until 1925. Train travel was from that time on uninterrupted from New York to St. Augustine. Visitors began utilizing the luxurious all-Pullman trains with closed vestibule cars and electric lights throughout. Even President Grover Cleveland made a visit via train to the Ponce de Leon.

A modern rail depot was another amenity provided by Flagler for his hotel guests and other visitors to the area. Built on 32 acres of reclaimed marshlands, he was proving that with vision and money he could indeed utilize land previously overlooked as wasteland.

By 1889, Flagler had most definitely put his past behind and with a vision for the future, pursued with all his wealth and talents, became builder and developer extraordinaire. As the railroad penetrated further south into what was a verdant citrus landscape, Flagler's enthusiasm only mounted as he sought another prospect, another hurdle. He was undaunted as the expansion grew to other regions. His name became magic and the potential seemed limitless. When Flagler bought out John Anderson and Joseph D. Price and took over their small hotel in Ormond Beach, he enlarged the hotel and enhanced the grounds by improving the existing eighteen-hole golf course. Flagler did not care to play the game himself but he knew what the attraction meant and soon proved that visitors enjoyed golfing as well as going to the automobile races — popular even then at Ormond and Daytona beaches.

Daytona became the southerly terminus for Flagler's railroad for some years, leaving the waterways of the Indian-inhabited banks of the Indian River, Lake Worth and Biscayne Bay, the main arteries for travel and commerce further south. The southern regions were agriculturally rich sources of oranges and pineapples and soon they too would become accessible, compliments of Henry Flagler.

In 1892 Flagler received a charter from the State of Florida enabling him to build a railroad along the Indian River as far south as Miami. The line would ultimately do away with steamer transport. His first expansion into the area from Daytona was to Rockledge. It was thought at the time that he would probably go no further south than Lake Worth which was considered one of the most desirable locations along the east coast.

It was in 1893 when Flagler's railroad, reached Rockledge via Titusville and Cocoa. It had been less than a year of engineering and building to complete the eighty miles of road. Flagler had now commanded the title of railroad builder as well as hotel magnate and every concerned citizen in Florida hoped his plans included their cities. He was busy working his way south, clinging as close as possible to the coastline. In spite of the need for major engineering with marshlands to be filled and sandy soil to be graded, the tracks went in, the steel weighing ninety pounds to the yard. Eau Gallie was gained in June of 1893 and by January of '94 trains were operating to Fort Pierce. It was March 22, 1894 when work was completed to a point across Lake Worth from a slip of jungle overgrown with palm trees and named Palm Beach. While it would be the terminus for Flagler's railroad for quite some time, it was only the beginning of a grand, glorious golden era. Palm Beach was about to be discovered and more importantly, developed, by Henry Morrison Flagler, a man who had proven himself by enriching and enhancing the lifestyle of every community in which he became involved. He built hotels, schools and churches. Wherever he built he established churches because he wanted to attract God-fearing, hard-working Christian people to his newly discovered tropical paradises all along the coast. The electric power plants that went in to support his hotels became the precursor to Florida Power & Light Company.

Henry Flagler had arrived in Palm Beach and the Royal Poinciana Chapel was soon to become a vital part of his life and the lives of future generations. Another light source would soon illuminate the tropical island.

First School House – Church

$\mathcal{E}$ARLY
PALM BEACH

Henry Flagler was not the first man to discover the enchanted island that we know as Palm Beach. The island, just a narrow slip of land separated from the mainland by an arm of the ocean called Lake Worth, was not called Palm Beach when it was first discovered. The lake was named for General William J. Worth by United States soldiers sent there before the Civil War to settle Indian troubles. The waters were full of fish and the island held an abundance of wild game. It was a bountiful untouched paradise, however dominated by mosquitoes. Bears were plentiful and had dug down to a bubble of fresh water which the early settlers shared with the wild animals. The bears also sustained themselves by going to the beach to dig for turtle eggs. With bears and panthers and other wild predators, the settlers had problems keeping horses and cattle safely corralled. It was a far different island in the mid seventies just waiting to be discovered.

The first known settler in the tropical paradise was a man named Lang, a Civil War draft dodger who built a cottage on the west side of Lake Worth where the central core of the city of West Palm Beach is prominently located today. Another settler in 1860 was George W. Sears who discovered an inlet while cruising southward along the Florida coast from the Indian River. Sears met Lang and announced that the war was over. Lang left the area, leaving Sears as one of the few inhabitants. In November of 1872 Charles Moore arrived, taking over Lang's cabin.

Anyone entering the inlet back then went through a shallow pass into a beautiful tropical lake, the shores lined with overhanging trees, jungle vines, and mangrove. Sears passed the word along of the wonderful secluded paradise and others came to form a settlement.

In 1876 Albert Geer purchased forty acres on the island for 85 cents per acre, or thirty-four dollars. For the next ten years he cleared the jungle and planted coconuts salvaged from the wreck of the Spanish Barque Providencia. It was reputed that Charles Moore also participated in the planting, producing thousands of palm trees that dotted the island.

In 1878 a post office was established to support the few settlers. The designation was "Lake Worth" and the first post master, V. O. Spencer, used a rowboat to visit the settlers around the lake in quest of signatures for the petition to the Post Office Department. The name Lake Worth did not become permanent. Within a few years there was a move led by E. M. Brelsford to name the settlement "Palm City" but that name was rejected. Gus Ganford, a visitor from Philadelphia, prospecting in the wild jungle, heard about the rejection and suggested that the community submit the name "Palm Beach." Since there was no other city in the United States with that name, in March of 1886, the name Palm Beach, Florida, was confirmed by the Post Office

Department.

Ten years after Geer purchased the land, a sportsman named Robert R. McCormick, of Denver mining and railroad fame, arrived on a fishing trip and, seeing Geer's work, proclaimed, "Truly, this is a paradise — the wilderness has been made to blossom!" McCormick purchased the tract for $10,000, turning Mr. Geer's initial investment of thirty-four dollars into a fortune. McCormick built a cottage on the land three hundred feet from Lake Worth on the south side of what is now Royal Poinciana Way, probably a dirt path if anything at that time. Declared the finest home in South Florida and completed in 1886, it was built of wood and decorated using Georgia marble, stained glass windows and a three-story tower, all of which arrived by the schooner Emily B out of Jacksonville. The mahogany staircase and railing in the two-storied cottage were fashioned from logs washed ashore from the Providencia as the Barque broke apart. McCormick ultimately invested thirty-five thousand dollars in the property, cultivating many varieties of tropical plants, including six hundred rose bushes. To the wonderment of his neighbors, he also had two hundred fancy chickens roaming the grounds — sweet meat for the bobcats and crocodiles prevalent along the lakefront.

The first religious organization of any sort in what was then the original Dade County area, was founded by the Reverend Alexander Burritt Dilley in 1884. Known as the Lake Worth Congregational Church, it was created by the Home Missionary Society as the only church from Hobe Sound to Homestead. There were no school houses at that time. Religious services were held informally by the colorful Reverend, who referred to himself as "Father Dilley", whenever he could raise a gathering of two or more people. He made his spiritual forays, after working during the week as a laborer, wearing a tall silk top hat which increased his height and visibility to over seven feet. Dilley's appearance added a note of urbane elegance to an otherwise austere pioneer existence in the swamp jungle of Palm Beach. The 'Reverend' often espoused his worshipful message on the beach to boaters just offshore.

A combined school house — church was erected by public subscription and built by pioneers Lainhart and Dimick in 1886. It served the schoolchildren during the week, the Congregationalists and Presbyterians on Sunday morning, and those of the Episcopalian faith on Sunday afternoons. This first building has been preserved and may still be seen in Phipps Ocean Park in South Palm Beach. For several years the arrangement proved sufficient. However, when the congregation numbered about 100 souls in the winter, the mere 22x40 foot building proved too small and Commodore Clarke offered his two-story yacht house until a proper church building could be built. The much-used yacht house was eventually floated across the lake and served the City of West Palm Beach as a Reading Room and Library from 1898 to the twenties.

It was reported that the early settlers were not too anxious to share their paradise with Henry Flagler when he first appeared in 1888. There was talk of a "mysterious stranger" coming into Lake Worth on his yacht and making notes. That was the same year The Ponce de Leon opened and it was Flagler's first sighting of the remote paradise. He left the area with the feeling that it was the most desirable location along the coast for future settlement. There were not more than a dozen or so houses in Palm Beach at that time.

It is not known or recorded why he didn't see McCormick's cottage in '88 but when an itinerant photographer sent Flagler a photograph of "Croton Cottage", he replied, "Why I didn't know there was anything that beautiful south of Rockledge!"

It was in 1892 when Flagler returned to the island, preceded by his agent dispatched to sound out certain of the pioneers about selling portions of their land. He was particularly interested in acquiring a one mile square section which began about four miles from the northern tip of the island. On the west side of the island, facing Lake Worth, he intended building a hotel and a railroad bridge to the mainland. On the eastern side of the island, the ocean side, he planned to build some cottages and perhaps another hotel.

Rumors of Flagler's visit preceded him again in February of 1893 according to an account credited to Sarah Geer:

> "What then comprised Lake Worth was buzzing with excitement. It was being whispered about that the great oil magnate's representative had been in the vicinity and that Mr. Flagler himself was on his way. The rumors were confirmed by the arrival of the 'great man' in March. Mr. Flagler's enthusiasm knew no bounds, and upon his return to St. Augustine he exclaimed, 'I have found a veritable paradise.' He had purchased our former farm from its subsequent owner, a Mr. McCormick, for the stupendous sum of $75,000 and immediately announced his intention of erecting the largest resort hotel in the world and the extension of the Railway to this section. He began to quietly acquire more land, and Palm Beach's first real estate boom was initiated, assuming proportions of an old-time mining town rush."

Flagler was reported to have paid $50,000 for a point of land owned by general store operator E. M. Brelsford on the sheltered side of Lake Worth. He also bought land along the ocean beaches. At Brelsford's Point, Flagler would later build a winter home. On the old Geer homestead, he planned to construct the Royal Poinciana Hotel.

The rush was definitely on. Land sales were publicized and real estate that had been virtually worthless jumped from $150 to $1,500 per acre. Homesteaders, numbering only thirty or forty in cottages scattered around the one hundred miles of lakeshore, suddenly found themselves rich.

To build the Royal Poinciana Hotel, Flagler's contractors, Joseph A. McDonald and James A. McGuire, immediately recruited hundreds of workers, putting up tents and shanties north of the building sites to house those coming into the area. The temporary quarter was named *The Styx*.

In May of 1893 work commenced on the hotel but progress was impeded due to lack of direct rail access. All materials brought overland to Eau Gallie were transported by boat to Jupiter, then transferred to the Jupiter, Lake Worth Railroad, constructed in 1889 and dubbed the 'Celestial Line' as it ran from "Jupiter to Juno by way of Venus and Mars." The seven and a half miles of track was maneuvered by an engine moving forward as it went south and chugging backwards on the return trip to Jupiter.

The financial cost of the line in rolling stock had been $70,000. The charge was twenty cents a hundred weight for freight and seventy-five cents for each passenger. When Flagler began utilizing the line the railroad collected over ninety-six thousand dollars in fees for hauling building supplies. Other materials arrived during the massive construction project, unlike any other that had occurred anywhere in the world, via river steamer south along the coast. To facilitate progress Flagler purchased several Mississippi steamers for that purpose.

Flagler set up a race between his railroad men, who were feverishly working to extend his line to the Palm Beach area, and his builders. Construction started on the hotel on May 1, 1893 with more than 1,000 men working, including some of the finest artisans of the world. It was soon apparent that 'The Styx' could not accommodate all the workers. Flagler looked west where miles and miles of open, well-watered land on the mainland seemed ideal for a new town "for my help." It was Flagler's concept to establish a commercial settlement on the west side of the lake leaving Palm Beach to the winter visitors. Obviously, the concept has had far-reaching consequences maintained to some degree to the present time.

In April 1893 Flagler purchased several hundred acres on the mainland, largely from Captain O. S. Porter, and laid out the city of West Palm Beach. He moved The Styx to the new town and in what resembled a mining town, more workmen poured into the area. Until the railroad bridge was completed the workmen rowed across

Lake Worth each morning to their jobs.

West Palm Beach at that time extended from the shore of Lake Worth west to Clear Lake and comprised streets named by Flagler for the trees, fruits and flowers indigenous to the area such as Clematis, Fern, Banyan, Lantana, Narcissus, Poinsettia, Tamarind, etc. Early developers to the burgeoning community were merchants George S. Maltby, a furniture dealer and undertaker from Kansas, E. M. Hyer from Orlando who opened a small general store and Captain E. M. Dimick, who owned the first drugstore in the city. J. E. Ingraham, one of Flagler's most able assistants, was placed in charge of the construction of the infant town.

One of Ingraham's first initiatives was to organize fire fighters. The shacks and huts and many of the early commercial buildings were of wood and highly flammable and 'Flagler Alerts' were assigned the vital job of answering when the fire alarm sounded. They jumped on bicycles, donned helmets and coats and then sped away toward the flaming structure pulling cart-like hose and reel and hand engine, hoping the fire would not burn out before they arrived. The day of the horse-drawn fire engine was yet to come to West Palm Beach.

While the hotel was under construction on the island, Flagler's influence in West Palm was also substantial. Gradually houses were built for his employees and the temporary dwellings were slowly torn down. It was even rumored that Flagler arranged for the occupants of the Styx to attend an entertainment performance and during their absence had the shacks burned to the ground. However, Flagler was more than generous and anxious for his people to enjoy the many wonderful attributes of the area and his provision included land for churches and even included a plot of land for a municipal cemetery. He eventually had an inscription placed over the entrance: 'Anything so universal as death must be a blessing.' It remains to this day a prophetic message of enduring solace. At one time he expressed a desire to be buried in West Palm Beach. He provided a lot on which St. Ann's Church was built, the first Catholic Church in what was becoming a growing community populated by 1,700 residents. As the growth continued Palm Beach County was formed in 1909 from Dade County with West Palm designated the county seat.

Flagler's greatest early contributions to the Lake Worth region were the extension of his railroad down the east coast and the construction of the Royal Poinciana Hotel and then The Breakers, initially called The Palm Beach Inn. The railroad was completed to West Palm on April 2, 1894, opening the "American Riviera by the Ocean", as it was then advertised in newspapers in northern metropolitan cities.

During the building of the hotels the Celestial Railroad was actively engaged. The short line had collected well over ninety thousand dollars for hauling supplies. However, the short haul railroad could barely keep up with the demand for services and Flagler bypassed the small railroad, putting it out of business and continuing his line directly from Daytona to Lake Worth.

The Royal Poinciana Hotel, named for the large rangy tree with the magnificent orange-red blooms, native of Madagascar and common to the tropics, was completed in record time and opened February 11, 1894. Located on the eastern shore of Lake Worth, it embraced about one hundred acres of the most beautiful land, the grounds covered with perhaps the greatest variety of tropical growth found in Florida. Deemed one of the largest wooden buildings in the world used for hotel purposes, its building statistics were staggering. It required 1,400 kegs of nails, 5,000,000 feet of lumber, 360,000 shingles, 4,000 barrels of lime, 500,000 bricks for the foundation, and 240,000 gallons of paint. There were 1,200 windows and 1,300 doors. In the building process part of the land had to be built up and Flagler's engineers dumped thousands of carloads of earth on marsh lands which would become two magnificent golf courses adjacent to the hotel. Avenues of Australian pines were also planted to enhance the property.

When completed the six story hotel was a sprawling structure filling the shoreline and holding 540 rooms. It would be enlarged to accommodate 1,200 guests and held a dining room with seating for 1,600.

The interior colors of the Royal Poinciana were green and white, the chairs upholstered in green velvet. The outside was painted yellow with white trim. In the center of the expansive

The Royal Poinciana Hotel, Palm Beach, completed 1894

building was a large rotunda from which ran several miles of hallways. There were spacious drawing rooms, lounges, parlors and a casino, and a large veranda across the front of the building. The tariff for a room in this magnificent hotel was a hundred dollars per day double occupancy including meals and it was to be opened for the season from December to April.

In the early nineties there were few homes on the island and the roads were hardly more than paths, except those laid out close to the hotel made of shell rock with a lane that ran to the beach. Some time after 1894 a horse car type of vehicle drawn by a mule carried the guests from the hotel to the ocean along what became known as Piney Lane running through the golf course.

The Royal Poinciana soon became the gathering place for wealth, fashion and society. It was known throughout the United States for its service and food. In addition to formal dining and parties, popular daytime activities included strolls amidst the gardens or along the lakefront, golf, tennis, boating and biking and riding about in wheelchairs (later referred to as Afromobiles). Afternoon teas and dancing under the stars at night in the Cocoanut Grove Tea Garden adjoining the hotel became salubrious pleasures.

The dress of the day was quite formal with long dark skirts and white leg-of-mutton long-sleeved blouses and high-button shoes for the ladies; the men wore light trousers or tight-fitting knickers, dark coats and shirts with stiff collars and caps or straw hats. The evening required more formal attire and with no such thing as air-conditioning, it was common for the ladies to change five, six and even seven times during the day. One can only imagine the luggage that arrived at the hotel and the labor of laundry performed for the wealthy guests.

'Father Dilley' retired to Denver in 1889 and Reverend Edwin J. Klock assumed the pastorate of the Lake Worth Congregational Church at about the same time when the first wealthy northerners began arriving and building their fine Victorian cottages. The Geer family residence occupied the property where the Chapel now rests. On April 8, 1891, Reverend Klock presented to the informally associated group a Constitution and Rules, thus beginning the first formal membership roll and registry of church business. This organization was called the Union Congregational Church on Lake Worth and was approved thusly. Curiously, it was considered important in those times to list in the roster whether the member had been baptized as infant or adult.

When Flagler began purchasing the property along the lake and building the hotel, he offered a plot of land adjacent to the hotel to the Congregationalists. He even offered to build a church which would be an annex to the hotel. Flagler wanted the church for hotel guests and felt that it should be nondenominational to appeal to a broader spectrum of worshippers. There was a battle of sorts to maintain denomination and the Congregationalists moved to West Palm. Soon after Flagler's arrival, most of the permanent residents had sold their east side property to his agents and had moved across the lake.

In April of 1894 the Missionary Society elected Fred Dewey, E. N. Dimick and George Lainhart as trustees, and E. M. Brelsford as Treasurer. Mr. Brelsford reported $1,457.36 on hand, and it was decided to proceed with the building of a manse, wharf and sea-wall on the property owned by the Society. Negotiations were being held with Mr. Flagler and his representatives as to what assistance might be obtained from them to build a church. At the same time the Union Congregational Church was built on Olive Avenue and Datura Street on Flagler-donated land and would be considered the "full-time" Church while the Chapel was the "Seasonal" Church. A supply minister from the Home Missionary Society, Reverend Isaac A. Pearce and Mrs. Ada H. Pearce, transferred their religious affiliation, by letter, to the Union Congregational Church at Palm Beach, on April 29, 1894. The registry of church business of that time records Rev. Pearce as being chairman, and it may be assumed that his pastorate began then.

When the island residents moved to the 'new town' the permanent membership in the Chapel, the genesis of the church we know today, dwindled to only six souls.

Reverend Pearce served both east and west side churches in what became an unpopular pastorate on both sides of the lake. Mr. Flagler then made it possible for the Congregationalists to sell the original lot, the funds from which, along with substantial anonymous donations, enabled the construction of the present Chapel. It was often difficult to identify Henry M. Flagler as the benefactor of the Chapel because of his reluctance to publicize his generosity. However, his previous record of great benevolence toward church groups and societies was legendary.

It was during this period when Flagler recognized a marked change in Ida Alice. Her conduct had become strange and over a period of months was becoming more pronounced. She was erratic and irritable and Flagler hoped that it would "not call for wide-spread notice." However, Dr. George G. Shelton, a prominent New York physician and personal friend of the family, was called when Ida Alice began speaking of her great love for the Czar of Russia, explaining that she had just been informed by the Ouija board that the Czar was also madly in love with her. Upon further observation Dr. Shelton was stunned. As she hallucinated, she divulged that the Czar planned to marry her upon the death of Flagler. Dr. Shelton became fearful for Flagler's safety and warned him to take every precaution. One can only imagine the anguish that was caused by this turn of events. When it became necessary to have Ida Alice committed to Choate's Sanitarium in Pleasantville, New York, Flagler's grief was palpable.

Dr. Shelton advised that Flagler go to Florida to remain there for the winter. Dr. Shelton felt that Dr. Anderson in St. Augustine could do much to mend his spirits. In a letter addressed to Dr. Anderson he wrote: "Mr. Flagler proposes to start for Florida next week. I have advised very strongly that he do that because he is almost prostrated with grief and anxiety. I have seen him in deep trouble, but never has anything taken such a hold upon him as this. I hope you will keep him in the south until the edge of his grief wears off ..."

There was always much in Florida to distract or at least occupy Flagler. Florida experienced its coldest weather in over a hundred years during the winter of 1894-95. The first freeze occurred on December 24, 1894, followed on the 28th by temperatures as low as 19°. In February of 1895 another hard freeze occurred. The citrus crop was devastated and vegetables and coconut palms as far south as Palm Beach were lost, resulting in property losses in the millions. Many permanent residents packed up and headed north. Confidence in the state and its potential for becoming a great citrus-producing region were in jeopardy. However, there was someone who had the confidence and interest, enough to inspire Henry Flagler. Her name was Julia D. Tuttle, a pioneer settler who was enjoying the warmth of Fort Dallas, later named Miami, while those people in the northern portion of the state were freezing. Also from Cleveland, Julia Tuttle may have known Flagler years before when he resided in the northern city. She certainly knew of his connection with Standard Oil and of his most recent developments along the eastern coastline. She contacted Flagler hoping that he might be interested in extending his railroad to Fort Dallas. It was in her interest that he at least begin to buy land in the area along the shores of Biscayne Bay.

Flagler sent J. E. Ingraham to investigate the conditions and was delighted with the report that the freezing weather had not reached that far south. Flowers were in full bloom and not a single orange tree had been killed. As evidence, Mrs. Tuttle and Ingraham picked some of the choice flowers and foliage, wrapped the stems in damp cotton and sent the bouquet to Flagler. Flagler was amazed and decided a trip to Fort Dallas was warranted.

The sixty miles between Palm Beach and the Miami River was unbroken wilderness. Mail was delivered only once a week, carried by a man who walked the entire distance. The Flagler entourage was not so ambitious and covered the distance from Palm Beach to Ft. Lauderdale by launch and from there rode in a cart drawn by mule on dirt paths the remainder of the way. It was an arduous passage at best through the jungle lands and, if nothing else, called for rails.

Mrs. Tuttle was persuasive in her argument to have Flagler extend his railroad south and even gave him one hundred acres of Tuttle land for a railroad terminal, rail yards and a hotel site. She retained thirteen acres north of the Miami River which today is the heart of the city of Miami. Flagler promised on June 12, 1895 to extend his railroad to Biscayne Bay, build a terminal, lay out streets and build municipal water works. All of these plans were occupying a man who was desperately concerned about the health of his wife.

Flagler's second Palm Beach hotel, located directly east of the Royal Poinciana Hotel, on the ocean shore, was built in 1895 and completed in January of 1896. The Palm Beach Inn would not rival the Poinciana until it was enlarged and the name changed to The Breakers in 1900.

Flagler also built a number of cottages along the ocean. In 1896 he had built a railroad and footbridge across Lake Worth, connecting the two Palm Beaches. This made it possible for visitors to come to West Palm Beach on his railroad and have easy access to either of his hotels. The tracks reached the Palm Beach side at a point just south of the Poinciana Hotel and from there continued on to the Palm Beach Inn. For several years trains deposited passengers at the south door of both hotels. Private railroad cars became prevalent, arriving for the season with sometimes as many as a hundred of the luxurious cars parked outside the Royal Poinciana and alongside the Inn. As the wealthy visitors arrived they seemed to relish the grandeur of the elegant hotels amidst the tropical lushness of a paradise being groomed and enhanced to enrich their winter hiatus.

The religious worship, so important to Flagler and obviously enjoyed by a growing number of visitors to the area, was in sharp contrast to another addition to the island. Colonel Edward Riley Bradley, partner of Flagler in the Bacchus Club in St. Augustine, finished building Bradley's Gaming House on property just north of the Royal Poinciana Hotel. The Kentucky Colonel, invited by Flagler to come to Palm Beach, spent his summers at Idle Hour Farm where several Kentucky Derby winners were sired. Edward Bradley and brother John constructed the unpretentious white frame building 1,000 feet north of the Royal Poinciana Hotel and incorporated under the laws of Florida as the private Beach Club. When the club became popular, after opening its domain to women, it was noted for its elegant dining facilities as well as for games of faro and roulette and it was heard to be said that, "With Mr.

Flagler's blessing, we have salvation in the south, and sin to the north." Bradley's Beach Club, after Monte Carlo, became the most famous casino in the world.

The Reverend Pearce had served both east and west side churches as supply minister from the Missionary Society. When the Union Church called for a permanent pastor, Flagler offered to provide the salary and accommodations to a minister of his choice for the hotel's short season, thus relieving the Society of the additional burden. Dr. Edwin B. Webb, a prominent ecclesiastic of the period, from Boston, was called upon. Dr. Webb was seventy-five years of age when he took the position in 1896. Dr. Webb was a forceful speaker with a friendly, kind demeanor whose sermons were of the highest quality. It was Dr. Webb who would fill the pulpit of The Royal Poinciana Chapel, and it was Dr. Webb's charge that he preside over what was still a Congregational service. The Chapel, as we know it today, was about to evolve. Its continuing evolution was to be directed by Dr. Webb, under the on-going influence and needful caring of Henry Morrison Flagler at a time of great upheaval in the 'Great Man's' personal life.

$\mathcal{F}$LAGLER'S
CHURCH

The Royal Poinciana Chapel that we know today was begun in late 1897 and completed in 1898. The Victorian Gothic style was referred to as 'Colonial' with rounded steeple attributed to a design styled after "Sir Christopher Wren." Often called a "Meeting House" it was built from plans by J. W. Ingle to blend with The Royal Poinciana Hotel. George Lainhart, early pioneer settler, was contracted to be superintendent of the construction at a salary of $4.00 per day.

The original site of the Chapel was in the Royal Poinciana Gardens, about three hundred feet from the entrance of the massive hotel. It was initially designed to seat four hundred. The services had become popular with hotel guests as Reverend Webb presided over the weekly Congregational service. He was a "sympathetic" preacher and laid the foundation for the future services in the Chapel. On January 26th of 1899 Dr. Webb spoke on "The Reasons St. Paul Went to Rome to Preach the Gospel." This was followed by "The Peril of An Empty Mind." His messages were forceful and provocative but there is no information to enhance our knowledge of how much time Flagler spent listening to Dr. Webb.

Flagler was engaged by many compelling issues and projects. As promised, he had surveyed the rail extension south from West Palm in 1895 and was over-seeing the difficult construction as labor camps were put in to support the arduous task. Steamers from the Indian River were used to carry materials and supplies the seventy miles to be covered, necessitating dredging portions of the inland waterway. As the rails were set several small towns were laid out. Flagler was instrumental in establishing small communities of workers in Delray Beach, Deerfield Beach, Fort Lauderdale, Dania, Hallandale and Ojus. When Flagler built a railroad station in Ft. Lauderdale in 1897 it became the most prominent town on the road between West Palm and Miami.

The railroad was completed to Miami in April of 1896 and people began pouring into the new city. The newest development only spurred interest in all of Florida, and Jacksonville enjoyed the benefits by setting seven days aside in the spring as "Gala Week." The New York Giants held spring practice in the "Gateway City" to Florida and the residents were singing a brand new song, "Take Me Out to the Ball Game."

It was September of 1895 when the name of Flagler's various railroads were changed by charter to the Florida East Coast Railway and signed by Governor Henry L. Mitchell. The change was propitious as Flagler had bought and accumulated enormous parcels of land all along the coast in order to put in his railroad. The new road became a Florida institution escaping Interstate Commerce Commission regulations which was beneficial to Flagler enabling him to charge higher freight rates.

Flagler was particularly sensitive to each of his new communities and desired to beautify every development with native flora. However, as he aged he tried to rush nature. In one instance it is reported that when the soil was not conducive to the growth of Australian pines, he had certain sections dynamited and rich soil transported by rail from Palm Beach to aid in the growth. His attention to detail was extraordinary at a time when personal tragedy was ever-present.

It was during the time when he was actively engaged in the railroad south and while the Chapel in Palm Beach was under construction when Flagler felt compelled to spend more time in New York. Ida Alice had been released from the sanitarium and the Flaglers enjoyed time together in Mamaroneck. Sadly her condition did not remain stable and she again had to be committed. She insisted her name was Princess Ida Alice von Schotten Tech, that she was previously married to Henry Flagler, but he was dead and she proposed to marry the Czar of Russia. Dr. Shelton arranged for her to return to the sanitarium in Pleasantville. No one could doubt Flagler's love for his wife as he sought the finest medical treatment available. When she was deemed beyond a cure, he knew their separation was final. Flagler had, for some time, contemplated divorce but he knew the storm of criticism it would bring. It was, however, illegal in New York and Florida at that time to gain divorce using insanity as the basis. He moved his citizenship to Palm Beach where he felt he would be more successful gaining freedom from a marriage that had long ago ceased to exist. His intentions were announced in the *Florida Times-Union* and the glare of media disclosure was painful.

It was noted that on January 26, 1899, Rev. Webb preached at the Chapel and that on February 28 of the same year Rev. Dr. Sanden of New York filled the pulpit. Dr. Webb was eighty when he died suddenly before the season of 1900.

The Congregational Society was overly burdened operating two separate churches, with construction bills of several years still unsatisfied. Flagler was asked by the Trustees to assume ownership of the Chapel. This was accomplished on March 19, 1900 and Flagler paid the Chapel's debts from his private purse.

The Congregationalists had prevailed since the beginning of Reverend Dilley's ministrations. The Congregationalists wanted the congregation to be Congregationalist. Mr. Flagler wanted it to be interdenominational to better serve his hotel guests who were of many different denominations. It was also Flagler's desire to provide a center of musical and religious culture which would parallel the wonderful services rendered by the hotel. It was, then, to The Royal Poinciana Chapel, an interdenominational Chapel, that he called forth Dr. George Morgan Ward, President of Rollins College, in Winter Park, Florida, to be minister for the 1900-1901 winter season.

Flagler's invitation to the young Christian leader was in a letter answered by Dr. Ward thusly, "... I don't want to give creampuff sermons to the idle rich." Flagler wrote back, "I received your sassy letter, but please come down anyway and let's talk." Out of that meeting, which was highly successful from Mr. Flagler's point of view, came the following five principles governing the ongoing direction of the Chapel:

1. The Chapel was to be interdenominational (or nondenominational) as stipulated at that time.
2. It was to have the freest pulpit in America.
3. It was to have the finest preaching in the Christian world.
4. It was to have the best music available.
5. It was never to have debt.

Dr. Ward agreed to serve for the season at a salary of $1,500, plus room and board for him and his wife. He would also continue as President of the college in Winter Park.

Dr. Ward quickly and assuredly found fertile ground in Palm Beach. Flagler's ongoing travail due to Ida Alice's illness was a constant heartache. The doctors had assured him that nothing more could be done.

In April 1901 a bill was introduced into the Florida State

Senate "to be entitled an act making incurable insanity a ground for divorce ..." When it passed, Governor W. S. Jennings affixed his signature on April 25, 1901, and the media accused Flagler of being instigator of the law. The public arousal over the divorce law brought condemnation to a man suffering remorse over his wife's irreversible mental illness. However, on June 3, 1901 Henry Flagler filed a bill of divorce against his wife. Doctors testified in his behalf that Mrs. Flagler suffered from a paranoia, otherwise known as chronic delusional insanity. When the divorce was final Flagler made provision for Alice and the financial statement was published in all the Florida newspapers.

A final divorce was granted August 13, 1901. Ida Alice was moved to a cottage at a private sanitarium at Central Valley, New York and from all reports was well cared for and would survive Henry by seventeen years, living in reasonably good physical health until July 10, 1930. She was eighty-two years of age when she passed away.

The incarceration of Ida Alice and the divorce had been devastating to Flagler. However, while still in the throes of seeking an answer to her malaise, he had met a woman who would bring some measure of joy to his life. Mary Lily Kenan was born in Wilmington, North Carolina and had become an accomplished pianist and vocalist studying music at Peace Institute in Raleigh. Flagler met her in 1891 and even Ida Alice admired the popular lady for her grace and elegant manners, witnessed at the shared social affairs in New York and Newport as well as in St. Augustine.

Mary Lily was thirty-four and Henry was seventy-one when they married on August 24, 1901 at Liberty Hall, in Kenansville, North Carolina. The typical old antebellum home had witnessed the births and rearing of dozens of Kenans. Amidst a grove of oaks, sycamores, and elms it was an idyllic location for a wedding. The couple went by private railway car to Mamaroneck for their honeymoon where messages of congratulation from friends gladdened the heart of the aging millionaire.

From the beginning of their union Flagler spared no expense, giving his bride everything that money could buy. She always wanted a marble palace and one was begun several months after they married. The Gilded Age estate, Whitehall, was built in Palm Beach in 18 months at a cost of $2,500,000. Located just south of the Royal Poinciana Hotel, it was to be the grandest home on the island set amidst lush flowering shrubs, palms and Australian pines. Broad marble steps led to the colonnade extending across the front of the building. Great bronze grille doors opened into the Marble Hall backed by the double staircase of white marble. The interior of the house, executed by the design firm of Pottier and Stymus, was created in typical Gilded Age fashion — the interiors were designed to resemble historic styles such as Louis XIV, Louis XV and the Italian Renaissance.

While Whitehall was being built, the Chapel was enlarged to accommodate the attendance which had grown measurably during Dr. Ward's first season as minister, creating the need for two services and more seats.

It is of note that the first organ in the Chapel was a Mason & Hamlin Vocalion and that a "Professor Kahn of Jacksonville" dedicated the new reed organ in December of 1895 during the Chapel's first wedding service. It is presumed that the first organ was still in use in the larger Chapel as it was criticized by Russell T. Joy and other organists as being "inadequate." "The superb orchestras from the Royal Poinciana and Breakers hotels provided ensembles to accompany the professional quartet during the seasonal Sunday services, thus relieving the Chapel of the need to install an adequate organ."

The Chapel was moved at that time to a position in front of the Whitehall, facing north, and was deeded as a part of the property and dependencies given as a wedding present to the new Mrs. Flagler. From the turn of the century the Chapel was known as the "Flagler Church."

"The Great Man" had built or contributed heavily to the support of many other churches. However, he expressed the desire to have the Chapel remain strictly independent of religious affiliations, so that it would be "the freest pulpit in the world" where creed and ritual would not burden man's religious experience. The Chapel became Flagler's favorite place to worship and he considered Dr. Ward his pastor.

In time there were many examples of George Morgan Ward's influence on Flagler. In Edwin M. Akin's history, **Flagler, Rockefeller Partner and Florida Baron**, the following excerpt is notable demonstrating the strength of God's servant in the affluent pastorate at Palm Beach and the impact on and acceptance by his earthly benefactor:

'In keeping with his attitude with what he had done for Palm Beach, Flagler tended to exercise more control over it than any other resort he had created. He closed the casinos and other amusements on Sunday. As for objections to his policy, Flagler stated, "If they do not like it they need not come. I am not asking their opinion in this any more than I consult them on my other affairs. Sunday is to be kept at Palm Beach. Its observance is one of the features of the place." On at least one occasion George Ward reined in Flagler when the businessman told the minister that the Royal Poinciana Chapel was part of the East Coast System. Ward immediately challenged, "I thought, Mr. Flagler, it was the church of the Almighty God. As such it cannot be part of any human system." Flagler responded, "You are right, and if it has ever in any other way been dependent it never shall be again."'

$\mathcal{D}$R. GEORGE MORGAN WARD

"Sunday is to be kept at Palm Beach. Its observance is one of the features of Palm Beach." So saith Henry Flagler to Dr. Ward concerning the Chapel. It was a significant statement, for Henry Flagler understood how vital to his very being was a relationship with his God, with his Chapel and with his Pastor. In spite of the travail, his had been a life of tremendous accomplishment and devotion to work in fulfilling not only his own ambitions, but in providing the same opportunities for many others.

Raised in an atmosphere of Presbyterian ideology, and always affiliated with a home church wherever he lived, he held the countenance of solemnity, and also humbled himself realizing the blessings that were his. He knew, too, after suffering great loss and personal tragedy that spirituality was an absolute necessary complement to his daily table. It is presumed that Dr. Ward spent many prayer-filled hours with Henry Flagler.

Born May 23, 1859 in Lowell, Massachusetts, Dr. Ward was, at forty-one years of age, the youngest preacher to fill the pulpit of the Chapel. He would serve, during the three-month season, for the next thirty years. He quickly raised the attendance in season from 100 to 1,300, hotel guests and year-round residents alike, who found the handsome, athletic, blue-eyed gentleman with booming voice, worthy of their listening ear as well as their friendship.

Dr. Ward's intellectual accomplishments were varied and included two years at Harvard. When he dropped out he tried his hand as a building contractor but that didn't last long and he entered Dartmouth, graduating Phi Beta Kappa. Dr. Ward studied law at Boston University and along the academic path involved himself in religious work as Secretary and Treasurer of the United Society of Christian Endeavour. He became editor of the Society publication 'The Golden Rule.' He decided against practicing law and worked for three years in the mercantile business before entering Andover Theological Seminary and obtaining his PhD. While at Andover he took a post graduate course in history from Johns Hopkins in connection with theological studies. He was ordained a Congregational minister at Kirk Street Church in Lowell in 1896.

Rollins College engaged him as President in the spring of 1896. The same year, in June, he married Emma Miriam, daughter of Rev. Franklin Munroe and Abbie Ranney Sprague. Dr. Ward commented on what they found at Rollins when he and his bride arrived at Winter Park after what had been a devastating, unprecedented freeze:

> "When we returned that fall, we found the Treasurer dead, the housekeeper married, and the Chairman of the Board of Trustees resigned. There wasn't enough paint on the buildings to protect their nakedness." (It is written that he had to use his own personal funds to keep the college going and that would be the

case on many occasions.) "Then February came - I always hated February - that February was the shortest month that ever existed because those bills had to be paid on the first of the month or I was done. During the night before the first of March, I told The Almighty that if He was going to save this college, He would have to do it himself, that I was done. The next morning there was a pile of letters. I opened the top one and out fell a check. The check for several thousand dollars was from Mrs. Frances Knowles of Massachusetts to continue the benefactions of her husband."

Dr. Ward's impact on Rollins College was immediate. Not only did he bring fiscal soundness, but he revived the spirit of the student body.

It was a financial boon to Dr. Ward when the request came from Henry Flagler to minister to the congregation of the small white Church on the trail. Dr. Ward was outspoken when he credited Flagler with providing "... the freest pulpit in the world. Early in my ministry, even before assuming the position, I said to Mr. Flagler, 'I do not think I am so constituted that I could talk soft nothings to the guests at Palm Beach.'" Flagler's answer, "Who asked you to talk soft nothings? Speak as you think right." "Yes," I said, "but are you and I both disinterested enough and big enough not to be influenced at times?"

Dr. Ward stated on another occasion, "... I asked him (Flagler) his purpose in Florida? Is this investment or philanthropy, or are you anxious to pose as a state builder?"

"That's pertinent enough," Flagler answered, "I believe this state is the easiest place for many men to gain a living. I do not believe any one else will develop it if I do not. This is a safe kind of work for me to do. I believe it's a thousand times better than your colleges and universities, ... but I do hope to live long enough to prove I am a good businessman by getting a dividend on my investment..."

Dr. Ward was perhaps defending Flagler when he commented about another benevolence that he had become aware of at the hands of the criticized capitalist:

"The great freeze of 1894-95 wiped out of existence a hundred million dollars worth of property in a night, and men walked the streets with stricken faces and discouraged hearts. The tragedy of that day no one save a Floridian can ever know. In other sections of Florida men packed what they could carry of their earthly possessions and worked their way back north, leaving their houses to the bats and the owls ... but in these sections a man was sent on a mission. 'Find', were his instructions, any and every case of real need where a chance to start again will be appreciated and see that they have that chance. The only condition I impose is that they do not know the gift comes from Henry M. Flagler."

It wasn't long after the Wards arrived in Palm Beach when the Flaglers took residence at Whitehall. From the outside, Whitehall was typical of great wealth and beauty. It contained on the first floor the Marble Hall, Salon, Ballroom, Library, Music Room and art gallery, Breakfast Room and formal Dining Room. The Dining Room was typical of the grandeur of the other rooms, its walls hung in green tapestry, windows draped in silk velour, the chairs covered with Aubusson tapestry and window curtains of rich Colbert lace, the mantel piece with depictions of fruit and game and all illuminated by chandeliers hung with Baccarat crystal. The Music Room held many fine European paintings and statues designed after the Louis XIV period. The pipe organ, an Odell tubular-pneumatic, was reputed to be the largest ever placed in a private home in the United States.

The Ballroom had few equals, its dimensions ninety-one by thirty-seven feet, with a mezzanine for orchestra at one end. There were handsome mirrors richly ornamented, divided into panels and placed between long windows. The Ballroom, richly decorated in gold leaf, held Boucher-style and Watteau-style panels representing the four seasons and giving the room a tone of the old masters. The draperies were in two shades of rose de Berry silk damask, the Baccarat chandeliers the same as in the grand salons of the fifteenth century.

There were sixteen guest chambers, all styled differently but in typical Gilded Age fashion, designed as period rooms.

The most brilliant social season for the Flaglers was the winter of 1901-02 at the Royal Poinciana Hotel before the mansion was built. However, when they finally moved into Whitehall for the 1902-03 season, the mansion became a mecca

Organist Russell Joy

FLAGLER MUSEUM ARCHIVES

for socially prominent visitors. There were stag dinners hosted by Mr. Flagler and the guest list held such dignitaries as Sir Gilbert Carter, Governor of the Bahama Islands, Admiral George Dewey, Elihu Root, cabinet member of Theodore Roosevelt, John Astor, Henry T. Sloane, Lyman J. Gage and many other luminaries of the day. One of the most welcomed winter visitors was the famous English actor, Joseph Jefferson, a witty, lovable character and it was in his company when Flagler was photographed in what was described as, "the only published photograph (of Flagler) with a smile on his face."

The Flaglers shared the common pleasure of music and weekly programs were often performed by Russell Joy presiding at the console at Whitehall and also in the Chapel. Organ music was featured at all social functions given by the Flaglers.

The highlight of every season was the Washington Birthday Ball held each February 22. There were outdoor events including regattas on the lake but the major event was described in an account in the *Palm Beach Daily News*, the newspaper at that time published in a small office within the hotel and financed by Flagler. The ballroom was likened to:

> " . . . a fairy grotto filled with countless miniature electric lights set in scores of gorgeous and immense Japanese and Chinese lanterns. The walls were lined with stately columns of palm leaves, ferns and branches. Having dressed in the rooms of Whitehall's second floor, (the guests) descended the grand staircase to be greeted by Mr. and Mrs. Flagler in the Marble Hall. The entourage promenaded through the Music Room and St. Mark's Hall arriving in the dazzling ballroom all a-glitter with light dancing off the Baccarat crystals. Strains of music waft through the house as fourteen Palm Beach beauties began the minuet opening this most spectacular of the Season's affairs."

According to the newspaper account a judge came as Marie Antoinette, wearing powdered wig and solitaire diamonds. Financier Fred Sterry wore a gown of hand-embroidered lace and Joseph Jefferson masqueraded as Rip Van Winkle. "Henry Flagler of the thick shock of hair and ever-present cigar was stunning in a dress of Florida East Coast Railway colors, a Martha Washington combination of colors trimmed with bands of miniature silk flags and a palm leaf boutonniere. The ladies' costumes were not mentioned perhaps being outshone by the male plumage. 'At such times it seemed that the 'Gay 90s' were perhaps nowhere gayer than in Palm Beach.'"

In contrast to the frivolous parties, so important to Mary Lily, were the compelling problems facing Flagler's employees as the rail extension began south of Miami and into the Keys. However, Flagler always tried to comply with every wish made by his wife. When she did not like the noise created by the trains crossing Lake Worth, she requested that Flagler move the railroad bridge. He had his engineers build a new bridge from West Palm to a point north of the hotel. The trains continued to arrive, unloading passengers and also the private cars of the wealthy. A small depot was built where Royal Poinciana Way is located today.

With so many demands on the aging empire builder, Dr. Ward's plain-speaking wisdom was a soothing tonic to Mr. Flagler. Dr. Ward was noted for his remarks as he lived by example: "Be worthy of my friendship and you'll have it. Be unworthy and you'll lose it." "I am no theologian, my beliefs are few and simple." "Be sorry for your sins, but sorry enough to quit them." "Be fit to live and fit to live with." He had a way of making Bible figures come to life. One of his sermons, "What Lack I Yet?" from Matthew 19:20, like others prepared by Dr. Ward, was known to evoke from a parishioner, "But the sermon, Ah! There's a gem!" The popular message about the rich young man discussing with Jesus the fact that he had to give his money away, was preached by popular demand thirty-two times with thousands of reprints made and distributed broadly.

Through all the years of living among the wealthy and providing luxury resort hotels, where social affairs and games of chance were the accepted norm, Flagler never imbibed in alcoholic drink and he didn't approve of gambling although he was instrumental in bringing Bradley's Beach Club to Palm Beach. His influence also affected a healthy, outdoor activity after an observation one Sunday morning when Flagler saw two of his friends flipping a coin. He challenged the activity asking why they were tossing the coin. They answered that they were deciding whether to play golf or to attend the Chapel. From that time on, the golf course was closed on Sunday and stayed closed every Sunday until after Flagler's death.

Mr. Flagler enjoyed sitting with his men friends on a special section of the Royal Poinciana Hotel's veranda. Since they told stories that sometimes stretched to the limits of credibility, they called themselves the Ananias Club. It was in the days before radio and television and people amused themselves by enjoying each others' tales and personalities. The group often included leaders of the day such as Chauncey Depew, famous Confederate Army Officer Colonel A. B. Andrews, who was also President of the Southern Railway, John Sinclair, President of Bowery Savings Bank and William Hester, owner and editor of the Brooklyn Eagle. Dr. Ward was the youngest member and the only one with a head of black hair and mustache amidst the grey beards. As the older men failed in health or died, it was his presence that kept the veranda group meeting and talking. Gradually the guests began to refer to them as the "Old Guard" and later, in 1918, they formally organized themselves as the Old Guard Society of Palm Beach Golfers.

People in Key West were more than anxious for Flagler's railroad to reach them. He had had his engineers do extensive surveys and he, too, made the trip to study feasibility of what he knew would be monstrously expensive construction. The decision by the federal government to build a canal across the Isthmus of Panama helped influence his final decision. When the way was finally made clear for the construction of the canal across Central America, Flagler began to seriously plan to connect Key West with the mainland. Elihu Root, Secretary of War and a friend of Flagler's for years, felt that our interest in the Caribbean would be strengthened considerably by the proposed extension.

On January 30, 1905, Flagler and a group of associates left Miami by steamer for a tour of the proposed route. He met with citizens of Key West and the town was, from that time on, buzzing with the excited news. *The Miami Metropolis*, official mouthpiece for Flagler, reported the announced plans.

Additional detailed surveys were needed, mappings of channels and observations of winds and storms were all vital statistics to compile. When Flagler announced to Dr. Ward that he decided to build the extension the minister remarked, "Flagler, you need a guardian."

It would be seven years of construction more difficult than anyone could have imagined or anticipated, setting concrete bridges over spans of water as much as fifteen or twenty miles in length. The arduous, impossible feat, required an average of 3,000 workers and at one point 4,000 were laboring hard to achieve the goal. James R. Parrott, President of the Flagler System, combining all of Flagler's enterprises in Florida, was put in charge of the monumental project. Camps were built and even hospitalization for emergencies was provided by first-aid stations along the proposed route. There were supply boats that made regularly scheduled trips carrying food from the depot in Marathon and fresh water was delivered daily on special trains with flat cars carrying enormous tanks of the vital liquid sustenance.

The massive undertaking required heavy equipment of all sorts. There were launches, river steamers, tugs, dredges, concrete mixers and pile drivers moved in along with derrick barges, locomotive cranes and dynamos for generating electric light so that the work could proceed day and night. Joseph C. Meredith was chosen as the construction engineer, having built a pier at Tampico for the Mexican Government. Unfortunately, Meredith, who wanted badly to see the project completed, over-worked himself, on the job daily from sun-up until late at night, and died in the process. However, his replacement, William J. Krome, a Cornell University engineering graduate, saw the job through to the southernmost U.S. city.

Another man, invaluable to Flagler in his later years, was William R. Kenan, Jr., brother of Mary Lily. A graduate of the University of North Carolina in 1893, he ultimately joined the Flagler System as a full-time officer after working for the Carbide Manufacturing Company in Niagara Falls, the German Acetylene Company in Berlin and the Traders People Company in Lockport, New York. He had met Henry Flagler before the wealthy businessman married Mary Lily, and had worked for Flagler earlier building the power plant at The Breakers. In addition he also installed the ice machinery and laundry and directed the work of the power plants at several other of the Flagler hotels. When Whitehall was being constructed, Kenan served as a consultant in connection with the vapor heating, electric lighting, water and laundry plant for the mansion.

As Henry Flagler became less able to manage the huge corporation that had become the Flagler System, he depended on the younger men, Parrott and Kenan who were making more of the decisions governing the over-all operation, and signing the checks and important papers associated with running the Florida East Coast Hotel Company and the Florida East Coast Railway Company.

Since beginning the Florida development, Flagler had chosen as his advisors the foremost landscape artists and architects and urged them to employ their highest skill wherever he built. His Florida hotels became the winter gathering places of wealth and fashion from the north and from across the seas. In addition to the hotels in Jacksonville and St. Augustine and Palm Beach he built the Royal Palm in Miami, the Ormond Beach Hotel, the Hotel Continental at Atlantic Beach, south of Jacksonville, and he bought the Royal Victoria Hotel in Nassau and established a steamship line between Nassau and Miami. When he enlarged the Bahamian Hotel he renamed it the Colonial. In addition to the hotels, old rail lines were purchased and extended, some of which branched inland tapping rich agricultural lands and commercial points on the St. Johns River and Lake Okeechobee. One branch of the Florida East Coast Railway was the extension from New Smyrna through Maytown. The line would not be completed until after Flagler's death, but was completed before he died to a small settlement he named Kenansville, in honor of his wife's family. The line would eventually extend to what became known as the Florida Everglades, the soil of which is composed of a rich peat-muck and it was from this region after extensive drainage and flood control engineering, that carloads of vegetables would be cultivated. It also ultimately became an important sugar producing area. In the early 1900s the Florida East Coast Railway handled large volumes of citrus and also pineapple, grown successfully in the central and southern portions of the state.

As Flagler's empire grew a special department was formed to handle the sales and management of his land acquisitions. The unit was incorporated as the Model Land Company. Other subsidiaries were formed such as the Fort Dallas Land Company, the Perrine Grant Land Company, and the Chuluota Land Company. Under the overall Model Land Company Flagler controlled extensive acreage from Jacksonville to Key West and contributed in large measure to the agricultural and industrial growth of the east coast and inland regions of the state.

While the Flagler System grew, and Henry Flagler aged, he delegated more of the responsibilities to his able 'lieutenants.' He continued to spend summers in Mamaroneck and the winter season in Palm Beach. With age his eyesight became dim and it was hard for him to recognize people except by their voices. However, he never lost his erect posture or dignified appearance, the moderate height and handsome face. His short white hair was neatly trimmed and parted in the middle, his straight classic nose and closely cropped mustache remained ageless characteristics of the man who maintained a mind that was clear and alert. As he became less agile he spent more time in the mansion and enjoyed visitors, particularly Dr. Ward who spent many hours with Mr. Flagler. It is reported that while "Flagler and Dr. Ward seldom agreed on anything," theirs was a deep and abiding friendship.

Dr. Ward brought to that relationship wonderful credentials and a learned, academic life experience so entirely disparate from the capitalist. Dr. Ward was honorary Vice President of the Florida Audubon Society, was elected Trustee of Atlanta Theological Seminary and while serving as President at Rollins had also performed as professor of Economics and Law.

At Rollins Dr. Ward found himself in a college regarded by some as "Yankee" and of classical learning, dominated by the Congregational Church. *The Ocala Banner* reported in May of 1897: "In church matters, Dr. Ward has been very liberal. Among the newly elected Trustees are to be found Presbyterians, Methodists, Episcopalians, and other denominations. Truly, Rollins cannot be called sectarian ... He has come into touch with the State Teachers and their various organizations, has engaged as professors and officials several citizens of Florida, and never again can it be said that Rollins is not of Florida and the Floridians, a distinctively state institution."

An ad for Rollins in the *Orange County Reporter* of September 1897 read: "In the first place it is altogether independent, nonsectional and nonsectarian, as is demonstrated by the fact that in its faculty and on its board of trustees are representatives of all sections of the country, North, South, East and West, and representatives of nearly all the leading denominations, so it is not under any denominational restraints, and is untrammeled by sectional bias."

Dr. Ward was obviously embraced by the Rollins students early in his administration as President. In the fall of 1896 he stepped off the train on arrival at Winter Park and a group of students greeted him with the college yell. It became a tradition whenever Dr. Ward returned. On one occasion several boys pulled the college surrey down to the Winter Park depot, intending to substitute manpower for "Old Kate." Dr. Ward reacted: "Now, boys, if you have been miscreant, or are in bad standing with the Dean or any other faculty member, your courtesy is not appreciated, while if you offer your menial and horse-like services as an expression of your regard for me, I am deeply obligated to you."

In 1904 Dr. Ward relinquished his duties as President and professor at Rollins and accepted the Presidency of Wells College, Aurora, New York where several buildings were erected and dedicated during his administration. The George Morgan Ward Scholarship Fund was established at Wells by the Class of 1909. He would remain at Wells until 1912.

His association with Rollins continued and he would return to the college with some regularity until 1930. When automobiles succeeded "Old Kate" and the surrey, the students drove to the last stop on the railroad line before Winter Park, invited the Wards to descend from the train, and lead a colorfully decorated horn-blowing parade of automobiles back to campus.

An earlier tradition which was encouraged by President Ward was that of all college picnics on the shores of Winter Park lakes gained by rowboat, bicycle, horseback, or "Shanks's Mare" and in the surrey drawn by "Old Kate."

The first official train to cross the Key West extension arrived in the southernmost city on January 22, 1912. Ten thousand people were present to see the first section arrive to a frenzied throng, yelling and cheering until the celebrants were hoarse. On the train with Henry Morrison Flagler was Robert Shaw Oliver, Assistant Secretary of War, representing President William Howard Taft. Numerous foreign embassies and legations were also represented including Italy, Mexico, Portugal, Costa Rica, Ecuador, Guatemala, San Salvador and Uruguay. General José Marti, representative of President Gomez of Cuba, was accompanied by a Cuban band aboard a gunboat.

There were brief ceremonies before Flagler made his way to the edge of the platform and briefly surveyed the huge gathering. He was feeble, his eyes weak and blurry, but a kind smile graced his face. The Mayor welcomed him and presented a tablet of silver and gold, containing a likeness of himself. A children's chorus composed of thousands of voices, singing patriotic songs, obviously touched the aging empire builder.

The Miami Herald enthusiastically called the extension the "Eighth Wonder of the World" and the *Florida Times-Union* proclaimed, "Today marks the dawn of a new era. The old Key West, one of the most unique of the world's historic little cities, is shaking off its lethargy and from today the spirit of progress and development will be greater than ever."

It had taken seven years to complete the 155.84 miles from Miami, seventy-five of which were over water, to reach Flagler's southernmost terminus. He had achieved the ultimate goal against detractors who labeled the scheme "Flagler's Folly." Dr. Ward had suggested at the onset that Flagler needed a Guardian. Flagler built his railroad and George Morgan Ward was his spiritual, earthly Guardian during the process and until the end of his days.

Flagler spent his final years in Palm Beach in the company of Mary Lily and some dear and close friends and Dr. Ward was surely one of his closest friends. Valet George Conway, an English lad in his early twenties, became a constant companion, reading to the "Great Man" and rolling him along the lakefront in a wheelchair. Flagler enjoyed the grounds of Whitehall, inspecting his flower beds planted abundantly in Maréchal Niel roses and he enjoyed children. Reputed to be a wonderful storyteller, the children watched for the white-haired old man and some walked along with him as he was wheeled alongside the lake. Often a white spitz dog belonging to Mrs. Flagler followed close behind.

There were several people who helped bring comfort to the man during his last years and perhaps no one offered more solace than George Morgan Ward. The minister paid regular visits to Whitehall, which had become less than a joyful place. The socializing had ceased for the retired capitalist and after the initial merriment, when the big parties were given during season, it is reported that a friend commented on the size and beauty of the mansion and Flagler answered, "I wish I could swap it for a little shack."

It was in the grand house that Flagler suffered a debilitating accident, falling down the marble stairs. Bruised and shaken, his right hip broken, perhaps precipitating the fall, he was never again out of bed. The fall took place January 15, 1913. While he seemed to improve the first few days after the accident, he never really recovered fully and in April, his lieutenants, Parrott and Ingraham were beckoned. Flagler suffered from the heat and was moved to Nautilus Cottage, located on the beach about two miles from Whitehall.

His condition had declined markedly in May when son Harry was called from New York. The boy had not seen his father since the wedding in 1901 to Mary Lily. He came immediately to Palm Beach but the dying man had lapsed into a state of unconsciousness and did not recognize his son. On the morning of May 20, 1913 at ten o'clock, Henry Morrison Flagler passed peacefully, as if in slumber, with George Morgan Ward at his bedside.

At Flagler's behest, the body was carried to St. Augustine where it lay in state at the Hotel Ponce de Leon for several hours before the funeral procession to the Memorial Presbyterian Church. The Reverend J. N. MacGonigle, former pastor of Memorial, read selections from Scripture of which his special friend had been especially fond. The simple service was performed in a church packed to overflowing with friends and family. Dr. Ward and the Reverend Alfred S. Badger, pastor of Memorial Presbyterian, also participated. The committal service was private for family and intimate friends and jointly conducted by Dr. Ward and Reverend Peyton Hoge, of Louisville, Kentucky.

Henry Morrison Flagler, after eighty-three years, found his final resting place in a mausoleum adjoining 'their' church, alongside first wife Mary, and beloved daughter Jenny Louise and her infant daughter. The Florida benefactor left a rich heritage as the creator of Florida's two major industries: tourism and agriculture.

No period of mourning was declared in Florida in spite of requests by prominent citizens throughout the state. Mrs. Flagler did not think that her husband would have approved of such demonstrations. Thousands of telegrams were received expressing sympathy and floral wreaths were placed around his vault, attesting to the love and admiration held for the State Builder throughout the nation.

The many symbols of genuine caring, blessedly, were in stark contrast to what Flagler admitted to his friend, T. T. Reese, President of the Farmers Bank and Trust Company, in April of 1906, "I have lived too long and have been a target too often to allow myself to be disturbed by the jealousy of others who have been less fortunate. I don't know of anyone who has been successful, but that he has been compelled to pay some price for success. Some get it at the loss of their health: others forego the pleasures of home and spend their years in the forests or mines: some acquire success at the loss of their reputation; others at loss of character, and so it goes; many prices paid, but there is one universal price that I have never known any successful man to escape, and that is the jealousy of many of the community in which he moves."

Upon Flagler's death The Royal Poinciana Chapel became a part of the East Coast Hotel System, governed by a Board of Trustees. Dr. Ward would remain the minister during the 'season' for thirteen more years, and his contribution to the Chapel would be spiritually of great import. The Flagler era had ended but his influence and his many contributions to the East Coast of Florida and to Palm Beach cannot be over-stated. And one of the most significant and sustaining contributions was The Little White Church By The Trail, its' pulpit filled by Flagler's Pastor, George Morgan Ward.

George Morgan Ward

$\mathcal{F}$LAGLER'S
PASTOR

As President of Rollins College Dr. Ward was described as a dynamic individual whose charm, indefinable but all-pervading, brought out the best in others. "He entered sympathetically into their need and gave of his best lavishly ... He made you feel that you had perfect freedom of access to him, that he would never hold you off at arm's length, that he would share with you the intimacy of his heart," so wrote the Rev. J. Harold Dale, who knew President Ward for thirty-four years. "He was severe in defense of virtue, but his faith in people stimulated an answering faith in those with whom he came in contact, and fired them to rise to their full potential."

William Shaw in 1924, in his history of the Christian Endeavour movement stated, "In personal appearance, he was of the Gibson type, with clear cut features, commanding presence, voice deep and resonant, and a platform ability that challenged the instant attention of an audience."

Dr. Ward was wont to say, "I am no theologian. My beliefs are few and simple ... I subscribe to the creed of my church." At the Chapel his inspiration and counsel were available to millionaires, townspeople and servants alike. Because he was eminently practical, knowing a business man's problems from personal experience, his message was especially significant for men of the business world.

Mable Tilden McKinnon wrote of Dr. Ward's spiritual leadership: "During these years I knew President Ward as a man perfectly exemplifying the saying, 'He was a prince of a man' ... He possessed real brotherly love. He never tired of his service to others ..."

In 1912 he had resigned as President of Wells College and in March of 1914 he conducted a memorial service for Henry Flagler at The Royal Poinciana Chapel. His message was based on his sixteen years as pastor and close friend of the deceased founder of the Chapel.

Dr. Ward returned to Rollins in February of 1916 accepting a one year Presidency and in 1918 was elected Chairman of the Board of Trustees, at Rollins. It was also in 1918 when he gave the commencement address at Florida State College for Women (now Florida State University) and gave the Commencement address at Rollins. He purchased a permanent home, an early 19th century historic residence at Billerica, Massachusetts and he spoke that year at the dedication of the new Society of Christian Endeavour building on Beacon Hill in Boston. Dr. Ward would continue as President at Rollins until 1922, when he was made President emeritus.

An article in the **Palm Beach Post** dated May 23, 1920, by Joe Earman, is devoted to Doctor George Morgan Ward under the heading "BIRTHDAY ANNIVERSARIES Occurring Today of Prominent Florida People."

'Dr. Ward was sixty-one' and it describes how 'he came

to Florida in the EARLY DAYS, inspired with a desire to do missionary work in the broad sense of the word.

He declined the presidency of a large and prosperous institution in the west, and accepted the Presidency of Rollins College at Winter Park, at a time when the trustees were fearful lest they must close the institution for lack of support.

His desire was to meet the immediate needs of Florida at that time, and make possible the education of the TWO OR THREE GENERATIONS of Florida youth who had no money to pay for their education. He freed Rollins College from debt, put it on a firm scholastic basis and left in 1904 only when forced to go north by the death of his babies and the health of Mrs. Ward.

He was called from Rollins College to the Presidency of Wells College, where his work is a matter of record.

He left Wells College in 1913 because of a nervous breakdown, the same year Henry Flagler died, and traveled abroad for two years. On his return to America, while on a visit to Winter Park to perform a wedding ceremony for one of his former pupils, he was asked to straighten out the tangles into which the institution had drifted. He ANSWERED THE CALL and devoted himself without salary to the rebuilding of the institution.

He is one of the very oldest pioneer educators of Florida and of the south. He has been recognized as such by honorary degrees from both the State Universities, the independent colleges of the state: also by Dartmouth, his own Alma Mater, for his standing in the State of Florida and the unselfish part he has played in its development.

He is pastor of Royal Poinciana Chapel at Palm Beach, and during each hotel season many of our people avail themselves of the opportunity every Sunday to hear this eloquent and gifted divine. His congregations are cosmopolitan, but among their numbers will be found men who control the greater part of the wealth of the world. We wish Doctor George Morgan Ward much happiness on this his sixty-first natal day.'

An article in the **Post** dated January 1, 1928 talks of Dr. Ward's career at the Chapel.

'Reluctantly, Dr. Ward came to a congregation of so few, yet so important, members. The Chapel so small, had as its' back yard miles of jungle land ... where now there are rows of decorative pillars.

Death, poverty, disaster, in all its destructive expressions, swept with a merciless hand over the state of Florida in 1894. Cold that literally froze the progress of the state into a dead standstill, shrivelled the soil and its products: frost withered the groves and buried the state under a blanket of chill despair that was not content with striking death to the land, but stretched out its icy fingers and froze hope.

Rollins College, which was frozen to inaction and made powerless to go on, was succored by Dr. Ward, who might well be hailed as a saviour to a generation that should probably have lost education, spirit and proper religious training had he not responded to their call.

And it is not difficult to believe that when Henry Morrison Flagler whose life is a long, great story of achievement, wired for Dr. Ward to come to Poinciana Chapel, that his reply was "No." But Mr. Flagler was persistent and Dr. Ward was insistent. And the end of the two forces was that Mr. Flagler was sufficiently persuasive and reluctantly Dr. George Morgan Ward left Winter Park and made his home in Palm Beach.

There is perhaps no more interesting Chapel in the entire United States than the small white building that is nestled staunchly in the shadows of the Poinciana. Here is a Chapel, that is absolutely interdenominational. It is not branded by particular creed and wears no stripe that might prohibit any creed.

Search for romance of history and tradition, there is a wealth of it imbedded in the wood of this Chapel. Wood that has spread under the direction, the labor and the love of Dr. Ward, who knows no reluctance toward his congregation now - except reluctance to ever leave.

One small room comprised the original Poinciana Chapel. A wing on each side was added several years after Dr. Ward came to the Chapel and his study and the Sunday school room - the first Sunday school in Palm Beach - was added but five years ago.

Yesterday Dr. Ward glanced around the Chapel - and in his mind, Dr. Ward 'filled' the Chapel with his old congregation, placing in the pews names that command respect and love.

He pointed to the place that for years had been that of Henry Morrison Flagler - he placed side by side Colonel William Hester, Colonel A. B. Andrews, John Sinclair - and his recollection made him diverge to the memory of the Ananias Club that held its classic story-telling on the porch of the original stretch of the Poinciana Hotel.

Colonel A. B. Andrews, Grover Cleveland's advisor, and first vice-president of the Southern Railway, Judge Horace Russell, the power and brilliance of whose mind is honored by New York and all over the world, Colonel William Hester, owner and editor of the Brooklyn Daily Eagle, who thirty years ago showed Dr. Ward the plant of the Eagle, including the 'morgue' and surprised him by pulling out a file drawer and showing Dr. Ward his own obituary notice ready for use!

But the Ananias Club is gone - the jungle land is gone - the old organ that rebelled and even in its day of accommodation groaned and sighed, is gone - and, all but a few of the twenty-five who came to the Chapel for Sunday service and gave Dr. Ward material for next Sunday's sermon by arguing, questioning and testing his words, are gone.

And, with each succeeding year that leaves its days of memories, Dr. George Morgan Ward sees a growth that more clearly defines and emphasizes the greatness of the man who first planted the seeds that have ripened into beauty, prosperity, progress - his own planting a tribute to his worth - Henry M. Flagler. And, in naming those who have established their names as pillars of great worth and power in the community, he forgot his own - Dr. George Morgan Ward.'

Another article from that era appeared in *The Palm Beach Times* and describes Dr. Ward's memories of yesteryear:

"One day I got a telegram from Mr. Flagler telling me Dr. Webb was sick and asking if I wouldn't come preach in the Chapel. I finally told him I would come if he would let me tell them what I wanted to.

It was only for five or six weeks then ... and only about 25 people gathered every Sunday morning in the first tiny Chapel.

The Chapel has been rebuilt once and added to once. It now has a seating capacity of 1,300 and there is seldom a Sunday that every seat is not filled. Dr. Ward still "tells them what he wants to," and they still seem to like it.

When Dr. Ward asked Henry Flagler, "What the

dickens he was doing this for" (the Florida development), he answered, saying he had faith in Florida and that he wanted to make it possible for many people to enjoy it as he had enjoyed it. He wanted something to do with his money, "It's too much to leave to my children. Not good for them."

"He was a great man, a great man. I'm afraid not many people remember it."

Dr. Ward talked of those dear early days. Of how he and everybody thought "Henry" was crazy when he talked of building the railroad to Key West. "We are gonna have to ship him to the booby hatch!" "He's just plain nutty," said Col. Andrews who knew something about railroads himself.

When the Chapel grew and grew Dr. Ward finally had to give up his active part in the development of Rollins College. He left Saturday for a visit there, as President Emeritus. But the work at the Chapel carried on in capable hands. The Rev. William James Campbell, D.D., came here from the biggest church in Youngstown, Ohio to assist Dr. Ward. He will preach again this Sunday to the group which is already learning to love him as they love Dr. Ward.'

Dr. Ward spoke to many people of power not only in the Chapel but at commencement ceremonies and to the congregations of many churches. On March 11, 1923 he preached before President Warren G. Harding and the Presidential party at the Chapel.

Marshall McDonald was a young boy when he came with his family to West Palm Beach in 1925. The Chapel was located in front of the Whitehall, facing north. Marshall's father taught the Adult Bible Class and Marshall attended Sunday School and remembered that there were fifty to sixty children crammed into a room off to the left of what was called 'the little Chapel.' The room was no more than twenty-five feet by fifty feet and there were teachers for various age groups all together in the un-air conditioned quarter. In Marshall's opinion, "In those days you didn't expect as much as children and parents expect these days."

"At that time the Chapel had been enlarged to a capacity of 960 and 500 chairs were often set out under the palm trees in front for the overflow congregation. With two Sunday morning services, attendance often reached a combined figure of 2,500."

In spite of the fact that Marshall's father taught the Adult Bible Class and his mother, too, was active in the church, the McDonalds didn't have any social contact during the week with Dr. Ward. Living in West Palm Beach placed the family, like many other attendees, separate and apart from the wealthy visitors and those inhabiting the Island. Dr. Ward primarily mingled with the people who lived in Palm Beach and those that came down from the north, folks who "we considered to be a 'cut above' - they were the elite, the members of the Old Guard."

Sunday School 1926

Young Marshall gives further witness to Dr. Ward, "talking to mother, a vivacious woman, who for several years was involved with the music at the Chapel. There was no choir but a professional vocalist, Marjorie Moulter, was hired to perform each Sunday and she stayed in our home. Mother had attended a conservatory for music and had taught piano before marrying and hoped that I would demonstrate musical talent. It hadn't shown itself or been pursued until Miss Moulter appeared and then I took voice lessons at the Chapel - we were without a piano at the house."

In September of 1928 a hurricane of enormous velocity, the winds over two hundred miles per hour, took the steeple off the Chapel and moved a portion of the north wing of the Poinciana Hotel. There were very few buildings not affected by the hurricane leaving a path of destruction and loss. The hurricane only further diminished people's confidence after the Land Boom of '25 resulted in a resounding Bust in '26. According to Marshall, "People who had enough money in the late twenties to move back north left West Palm - leaving those of us who were not financially capable of making a dramatic move or change in lifestyle. We were stuck and most people who lived around us were similarly mired in a weak economy which was only further damaged by the Stock Market Crash of '29. The banks closed and real estate deals gone sour left start-up construction abandoned and streets with the beginnings of sidewalks unpaved for a long time."

Marshall McDonald's recollection of his youth gives insight to some of what occurred as other churches became established in the area. When he discovered girls his interest in the Chapel waned and he began spending most Sundays at Holy Trinity Episcopal Church in West Palm where the attendance of young girls was more pronounced. It is where he sang in the choir as "a mercenary." The Episcopal church paid Marshall and the other members a nickel every time they participated in the choir until Bethesda was built. When the new Episcopal Church on the island was completed, requiring an instant boys choir, they raided Trinity and offered each boy a dime to sing, even at rehearsals.

However, Marshall's musical career was short-lived. When he went to college he joined the Glee Club and held the honor of best attendance. In spite of financial straits, his parents purchased a tuxedo for the young student at a time when the Glee Club at the University of Florida held more prestige than the football team. He describes, "on a comparative basis, the Glee Club was better than the football team! However, when they began having individual auditions, they learned what was wrong with the second tenor section and it was me ... that Marshall's second register, *didn't!*"

While the nation was suffering the after-shocks of economic collapse, Dr. Ward was reducing his itinerary and there were assistants and other preachers who filled the pulpit of the Chapel. It was during Dr. Ward's last years when a quiet man sat in his audience, a man who would serve the Chapel significantly as time went on. His name was Adam Sarver, a layman who was not so much noticed at the Chapel as he was by his golfing buddies. He was called "Uncle Ad" and would be the glue to hold the Chapel together during a period of transition, instrumental in bridging the gap between the great preachers of the past and those of today.

Born Adam H. Sarver, in 1867 in Butler, Pennsylvania, he was reared and educated and taught school in the small town north of Pittsburgh. According to Sarver's great nephew, retired Brigadier General Richard P. Scott, 'Uncle Ad' sold buggies in the early years and later became close friends with Will Durant who was in the process of organizing General Motors. Sarver's intelligence, humor and executive ability attracted Durant, who took him to Detroit where he ultimately earned "bushels of money." When at fifty he developed serious heart problems he was forced to take early retirement. However, 'Uncle Ad' continued to be active in the Presbyterian Church, the YMCA, and the Boys Club in Pennsylvania and came to Palm Beach in the wintertime to play golf at The Breakers with the Old Guard Society. He began attending the Chapel and enjoyed the wisdom of Dr. Ward.

As Dr. Ward stepped back, he turned the pulpit over to such preachers as Hugh Black, minister of the Presbyterian Church in Montclair, New Jersey and a native of Scotland. In the March 22 issue of the **Palm Beach Independent** an article by Joe Earman appeared:

"It is not often in the religious history of Palm Beach County that a church edifice cannot seat the crowd.

On Sunday last the SRO sign, 'on orders of the Fire Department,' was displayed by the doors of the Poinciana Chapel which were closed before the service started. It is estimated that several hundred people were turned away. TWO CELEBRITIES EXPLAINED IT.

A PREACHER AND A SINGER.

Madame Honer, prima donna or Grand Opera singer, sang three hymns, the last one being, 'Just As I Am Without One Plea,' in which the congregation joined in the last verse.

Dr. George Morgan Ward was on hand and in his pulpit. He CUT HIS EYE at that great concourse, which SEEMED TO INSPIRE HIM, and then he prayed. His prayer was indeed a gem. He started with these words: 'Dear God have mercy on humanity,' and if there was any person in Palm Beach County or in the world that was not included in the beautiful prayer,

Josephus could not figure who was omitted.

He introduced the preacher of the day, Hugh Black, A Scotch Presbyterian.

He did not preach from a text.

According to my understanding, he expounded the Gospel as pertaining to ADVENTURE AND FAITH.

Doctor Ward preaches to the MASSES.

Doctor Black either preaches to the CLASSES or the HIGHBROWS.

In his sermon Doctor Black PREDESTINED in a few

GENERALITIES.

Like all high-brow intellectuals, he is nervous and being so full of his wisdom and a desire to EXUDE it faster than his tongue can wag, it creates a situation that can be termed 'CONTROLLED NERVOUSNESS.'

He had a vocabulary of CHOICE WORDS that SKINS anything that I have ever heard before in my life.

But at that I really do like the pure Gospel as preached by George Morgan Ward, who raps the sinful, (whether they be) the rich gang that come to Palm Beach."

Dr. Ward had been actively engaged both at Rollins College and Palm Beach through 1929 and for most of 1930. On February 24, 1930, he gave the Annual Convocation Address at Founders Week celebrating Rollins' Forty-fifth Anniversary. In the last years he had received calls taking him from his home in Bilerica to make long trips to officiate at marriages and funerals. He had been granted leave of absence to make a trip to the Holy Land to complete some research work into the Mosaic laws begun several years before. He was unsettled in his mind as to whether he would make the trip and return to Palm Beach, at least to start the season, and to greet 'his people.' His devotion to the calling in Palm Beach can best be rooted in his devotion to a task assumed in 1900 at the behest of Henry Flagler, who died in the arms of 'his pastor', Dr. George Morgan Ward. The minister never entirely recovered from the loss he felt at that time.

After opening the Chapel on Sunday, December 21, Dr. Ward collapsed with a heart attack after preaching. He was in bed at The Breakers Hotel, the following Sunday, when good friend Dr. William E. Biederwolf attended to the morning service. Dr. Biederwolf, ready to conduct the service, was notified that Dr. Ward had died shortly after 11 o'clock. The minister chose to withhold the announcement until after the sermon, when he quietly announced that the seventy-one year old minister, who had served the Chapel for thirty years, had passed away. The congregants were stunned and throughout the church there were gasps and then sobs as the parishioners moved slowly from the small white church.

His death brought eloquent eulogies from many different institutions and from humble individuals from all parts of the country and from every strata of society, for Dr. Ward spoke to every man.

Almost immediately the Board of Trustees of the Chapel extended a call to Reverend Biederwolf to become their minister. It was Dr. Biederwolf who presided over the funeral for the beloved minister on December 30 at the Chapel.

The funeral was for a man who had come to the Chapel, not to preach to the wealthy, but to all who came to "a Florida opened by Henry Flagler for all the world to enjoy." Dr. Ward was not so anxious to preach to the wealthy parishioners of Palm Beach when he preferred his task as President of a "penniless institution," which became a fully-funded, well-known Rollins College. Dr. Ward always spoke of "The Flagler Traditions" of "decency and a reverent Sunday observance." "There's nothing of the blue nose or blue laws about it", he was wont to say, "If I lived in a place where men worked all day for six days, I'd probably feel differently. But if men play golf six days a week, don't they need a change?" Dr. Ward supported the closing of the golf course on Sunday but pronounced himself perplexed as to the origin of the rule enforcing stockings for beach wear on The Breakers-Poinciana Beach. He regretted the passing of the use of the "Doxology" at the close of Sunday evening concerts at the Poinciana. He was too keenly interested in life to spend more than a passing moment in regret for the "good old days" when he and the "chief" and "Joe Jefferson fished off the pier and caught such unusual specimens as sailfish that had to be sent to the Smithsonian Institute to be classified."

George Morgan Ward was most definitely a man's man and among those who ushered at his funeral were William Fremd, George Neumann, Jack Crawford, H. A. Weatherby, William

Harding, Marshall McDonald, Sydnor Tucker and Ira Letteney, according to the Post's edition of December 31, 1930 under the heading GEORGE MORGAN WARD IS PAID LAST HONORS AT FUNERAL SERVICES.

'From the ranks of the Chapel trustees, the Old Guard Society, and personal friends a long list of honorary escort was chosen. (Among those were) J. Leonard Replogle, Gurnee Munn, H. E. Bemis, Henry Sloane, Harry F. Oakes, Jerome Wideman, Edward L. Arnold, William Newcome, Charles Walton, Charles M. Fuller, J. Field Wardlaw, Dr. A. G. Wardlaw and Dr. J. C. Fahnestock.

Composing the honor guards who stood watch all Monday night over the body of the deceased pastor at the Chapel were: George Neumann, F. W. Fremd, Jr., S. P. Hadley, Frank Koenig, J. C. Brantley, R. Blair, Jack Ecklund and Frank Young.

'Carry On' was the watchword of Dr. Biederwolf's short talk, in which he urged that those who had loved Dr. Ward "carry on" the work the minister had begun, that his influence might be lasting. From Mrs. Ward Dr. Biederwolf brought the message of hope that her husband's death might accomplish that which his life had been unable to do.

The music was simple in keeping with Dr. Ward's personal tastes. As an organ prelude Mrs. Clinton W. Effinger played old hymns. John Charles Thomas, baritone, sang Dr. Ward's favorite, "Oh, Love That Would Not Let Me Go", and the choir sang, "Nearer My God to Thee", and at the close a verse of "Steal Away to Jesus." The Chopin Funeral March was used as a recessional.

Mrs. Ward left at 11:50 p.m. to accompany the body of her husband to Lowell, Massachusetts where burial services will be held. She will return later in the season.'

On January 2, 1931 the burial service was conducted by Reverend J. Harold Dale at the Eliot Union Congregational Church in Lowell, with interment at Lowell Cemetery. On February 5th, a memorial service was held at Rollins College with the Royal Poinciana Chapel Choir assisting. A carved pulpit to honor the beloved minister and college president was installed in the newly built Knowles Memorial Chapel at Rollins and looking ahead, in 1957, the George Morgan Ward Memorial Park, in Winter Park, would be dedicated comprising a forty acre community recreation center to be enjoyed by many for many years to come.

The pulpit at the Chapel held Dr. Ward's presence and his inspiration for thirty years. He had spoken eloquently to Henry Flagler and to so many prominent people, to those who came from distant places and from across the lake to hear the words of the dynamic individual with the "Golden Personality." While he would be greatly missed and always remembered, he would be replaced by another dynamic "evangelist" from Winona Lake, Indiana, whose reputation extended not only over the entire United States and Canada but to many foreign countries.

$\mathcal{D}$R. WILLIAM EDWARD BIEDERWOLF

"Although the people of Chicago are presumably at least as much in need of a spiritual and moral awakening as the people of Palm Beach", (according to a February 8, 1931 Post article entitled BIEDERWOLF RETIRING AS ACTIVE EVANGELIST TO WORK INSTEAD WRITING, PREACHING HERE), "Dr. William Edward Biederwolf may be forced to renounce an opportunity to tell Chicago that machine gunners do not inherit the earth."

"Dr. Biederwolf, known all over the world as an evangelist, is the new pastor of the famous Poinciana Chapel in Palm Beach."

"Not only will Dr. Biederwolf probably have to give

up an opportunity to appear in Chicago, but also he will be forced to virtually retire as an active evangelist, in order to carry on his new work."

"When the sudden death of Dr. George Morgan Ward, pastor of the Poinciana Chapel for 30 years, brought the call for Dr. Biederwolf to accept the local pastorate, he was on the eve of starting a campaign for 'a moral and spiritual awakening' in Chicago, prior to and continuing through the World's Fair. Now he fears he will be unable to handle this work."

"Dr. Biederwolf is using no fiery methods in conducting his pastorate, but will revert to the more solemn tactics he adopted when he was a young graduate of a theological seminary and accepting his first pulpit in a little Indiana town."

"Dr. Biederwolf is an American-born citizen, a graduate of Princeton University and of the Princeton Theological Seminary. In school, he was conspicuous in athletic activities, notably football, gymnastics and bicycle riding. He was an expert on the horizontal bars and traveled with the Princeton team in exhibitions."

"After his seminary work, young Biederwolf accepted a pastorate in Logansport, Indiana, where he stayed for five or six years. He then served as a chaplain during the Spanish-American War and after this went into evangelistic work."

"Dr. Biederwolf has conducted campaigns and Bible conferences in virtually every state in the union and most foreign countries. He has been around the world three times and is especially well known in the Orient. In Korea, a leper colony bears Biederwolf's name because of the part he has taken in that work. He is a director of the Mission to Lepers."

"The evangelist is perhaps best known as director of

the 'World's Greatest Bible Conference' at Winona Lake, Indiana. He is also director of the Greenwood Lake Bible Conference in New York as well as the Stony Brook Conference on Evangelism."

"Author of 27 books on religious subjects, Dr. Biederwolf expects to continue his writings and spend a large part of his time on them, when not at his winter work in Palm Beach. His latest book, *The Adventure of the Hereafter*, was a best seller in the religious field last month."

"The evangelist expects to find great opportunities in Palm Beach and feels that 'the people of Palm Beach will respond to a message of the right sort.' He says he expects to preach nothing but historical Christianity."

"Dr. Biederwolf will divide his time largely between Palm Beach and Winona Lake, Indiana, spending four months there and three months here of each year. The rest of the time he expects to devote to writing."

"The work at the Poinciana Chapel will be carried on in an undenominational way, as before, the evangelist asserted, saying that he will offer a high grade character service such as should appeal to the residents of this resort."

" 'The people of Palm Beach need no different teaching than the people of any other city,' he asserted, 'for an individual is an individual rich or poor, and has the same spiritual needs.' "

The *Post* article referred to many of the outreach programs that Dr. Biederwolf supported and initiated and gave good reference to how the evangelist planned to occupy his time. One can just imagine the athletic minister as he impressed a young boy, a member of the congregation at the Chapel.

James Y. Arnold, Jr., whose father was Chairman of the Board of Trustees, was a boy of fourteen when he first became involved working industriously under Dr. Biederwolf's ministrations. Jim's father and grandfather were both ushers and they pressed young Jim into service. It became the young man's responsibility to set up chairs outside the Chapel. Jim has a recollection that on several Sundays "there were three hundred chairs - folding chairs of wood that had to be pulled from a room behind the Chapel and some from the old Poinciana Hotel. It was a heavy labor to gather, set the chairs in place for the service and then stack them to be put away. There were speakers outside providing the audible transmission of the sermon to be heard by the over-flow crowd."

When Jim was called upon to usher he remembers, "the adult ushers all wore white suits and were assigned to various doors. Father worked the front door and grandfather had the northwest door ... I was about fifteen at the time and I was in charge of the outdoor ushering and passing the plate for collection." He recalls vividly that when Dr. Biederwolf initiated the collection each week he never failed to preface the request with, "We will now have our SILENT offering", inferring that he preferred bills to the jingle of coins.

Dr. Biederwolf spoke at different churches in the area and young Jim's father often drove the minister. He recalls one meeting in Lake Park where Dr. Biederwolf spoke at length and with fervor about a treatment for leprosy, something called "moogra" oil. Jim says that "Dr. Biederwolf went on and on, as was his style, to pound the lectern and charge back and forth like a Princeton football player."

His congregants quickly learned that the minister's 'short' sermons lasted for an hour and if he really got enthused about his subject, like the leper colony in Zimbabwe, he could go on for an hour and a half. Whether he spoke to an outdoor gathering or from the pulpit, reputedly he wore black robes and worked himself into a heavy perspiration.

The Evangelist had traveled the world and that at a time when travel was far more rugged than in this day. He spoke of those travels and was a spellbinder. He described the crude living conditions in Capetown and in India and the arduousness of lengthy sea passage.

Dr. Biederwolf had many ardent fans and Dr. Howard Lee was one. Dr. Lee, while in seminary in Indiana, had to go out and practice preaching among the farming community and would 'borrow' some of Dr. Biederwolf's printed sermons. He said, "Every time I gave a Biederwolf sermon, people came to me and said, 'Mr. Lee, that was the finest sermon I ever heard'," and Howard pretended that it was his very own.

Young Marshall McDonald remembers Dr. Biederwolf as a "typical German, a highly opinionated man who had the robust appearance of someone who might enjoy the revelry of the beer halls. A famous evangelist, he was flamboyant when compared to soft-spoken Dr. Ward."

Margaret (Mrs. James) Waddell, had been raised in West Palm Beach. Daughter of a Methodist Supply Minister, she recalls vividly "driving over with my parents to hear Dr. Biederwolf preach. Father was very excited on those occasions and I enjoyed hearing the music played by Homer Rodeheaver on his trombone, all to a packed sanctuary ... there were even people sitting in automobiles listening to the service over a public address system. Father had all of Dr. Biederwolf's books and sermons. They were valued possessions for years until I finally gave them to a minister friend."

Another article in the **Post** gave further insight to the character of the man:

> "If you didn't know already, what sort of man would you think the person is? (referring to a photo of Dr. Biederwolf). Doctor, lawyer, merchant, chief? A bridge expert? A world traveler?
>
> Whatever you guess, you'd probably be wrong, unless you were an expert character reader. But that's what George Henri Lâ Barr is - an expert character reader. Mr. Lâ Barr can look at a man's face and tell him

what time it is, how much he pays for his shirts and whether he likes spinach.

Dr. W. E. Biederwolf, who, as everybody knows, is pastor of the Poinciana Chapel in Palm Beach. Here's what Dr. Lâ Barr had to say about him:

'The picture shows that the gentleman has a great deal of spiritual understanding and appreciates practical morality and high ideals of life. This gentleman's face shows that he has a great understanding of human nature and would make a good psychologist, a teacher, lecturer or a minister. He has also a great deal of intuition, the power to size up people by the impression they will make on him when he meets them for the first time. That is a gift. While he is a good disciplinarian, he knows intuitively human frailties and will make allowances. But woe to him who will try to do any smart aleck business with him. He could be stern, firm, and even stubborn, if forced. He is very dependable and will work for the uplift of humanity and for the betterment of the community. He looks like a business man, although his calling would be along educational, character-building and spiritual lines. He has a great deal of power of oratory in him and will make himself very clear; he wouldn't mince words and would pretty near call a spade a spade. In other words, he isn't afraid of anybody, dead or alive, and is very courageous in his convictions. Much more could be said of him, but due to lack of space we'll let it go at that. To sum up:

His eyes, keen observation;
His nose, positiveness;
His mouth, firmness;
His chin, stick-to-it-iveness.'"

Another article appeared in the **Post** describing some of what consumed Dr. Biederwolf's time while in Palm Beach and while away from the tropical paradise.

"Dr. W. E. Biederwolf, who recently returned to Palm Beach after an active summer in religious work in the north, on Sunday will begin his third season as pastor of The Royal Poinciana Chapel. At 11 o'clock he will preach at the initial services of the winter, taking as his topic for a Christmas sermon, 'International Peace.'

This summer Dr. Biederwolf divided the greater part of his time between his home at Monticello, Indiana, and Winona Lake, Ind., where for years he has conducted summer Bible conferences, with brief trips to Pennsylvania and New York for other conferences. In the fall Dr. Biederwolf, who has devoted the greater part of his theological career to evangelistic work, was in charge of an interesting evangelistic service at Wheaton College, Illinois.

Much of the summer Dr. Biederwolf spent in writing, completing two religious works for his publishers: "A Critique on Divine Healing" and "Illustrations from Literature", in which he draws religious truths from the great literary works.

In returning to Palm Beach, Dr. Biederwolf expressed himself as optimistic over the coming season and enthusiastic about Florida. Dr. and Mrs. Biederwolf have taken a home for the season at 162 Chilian Avenue."

On February 14, 1937 a memorial service was held at the Chapel for Dr. Ward, with the Rollins Chapel Choir taking part and it is presumed that Dr. Biederwolf presided in the pulpit. That same year he gave a sermon on April 4th, announced in the program under the heading Royal Poinciana Community Chapel (Sermons by William Edward Biederwolf), and entitled 'Public Enemy Number Six GAMBLING' - this at a time when the activity at Bradley's Beach Club was an accepted form of entertainment on the island and a highly popular pastime with the winter visitors, many of whom attended the Chapel.

The written sermon, if given in its entirety must have been one of Dr. Biederwolf's lengthier discourses with excerpts here that speak harshly of the evil activity:

'"They Said Therefore Among Themselves, Let Us Not Rend It, But Cast Lots For It, Whose It Shall Be." John 19:24

Within the shadow of the Cross casting dice over the garments of the dying Christ! Who but a gambler could be so dead to the eternal fitness of things and to the finer sensibilities of the human soul as to do a thing like that!

No man who is both good and wise has ever spoken one word in defense of gambling ... the best thinkers and most experienced observers in every sphere of life - statesmen, economist, literary men, as well as the clergy, have denounced gambling with unsparing vehemence as one of the most monstrous sins of modern society.

George Washington said, "It is the child of avarice, the brother of iniquity, and the father of mischief."

Charles Kingsley said, "Morally, it is unchivalrous and un-christian; the Devil is the only father of it."

Chauncey Depew said, "It is the one vice which seems to destroy immediately the moral sense."

Horace Greely said, "The darkest hour in the history of any young man is when he sits down to study how to get money without honestly earning it."

Were the opinions of these and all other great and good people wrong about this matter, or may it not be possible that those of us who give our approval and our patronage need have a renewed and a quickened conscience about it? Gambling has been very much on the

increase in recent years and no small amount of effort
is being made to make it legal and respectable.

At one time the French Government supported
itself by gambling house revenue. The harbors of
England were built through a lottery held at the front
door of Saint Paul's Cathedral. Yale and Harvard both
did the same thing to secure some much needed buildings. During Revolutionary days it was the common
diversion of what was known as the best society both in
England and America.

But as the years went by there came the ever-
increasing conviction that gambling is morally reprehensible, and with an awakened conscience laws were
passed in most civilized countries declaring the practice to be a crime.

The *Chicago Evening American* said, "Public
gambling, on the race track or anywhere else, is an
insult to the Constitution, an offense against morals
and common decency. It means the deliberate encouragement of degradation, and it will be stopped everywhere in the Unites States eventually, and in the state
of New York very soon - and that is well known to the
wise insiders among the Jockey Club "gentlemen", who
are selling their race horses and stock in race track
companies as quickly as they can find fools to buy
them." Yes, but that was April 24, 1908.

One of the crowning achievements of Chief Justice
Hughes when he was Governor of New York in 1908 was
a constitutional provision prohibiting race track gambling. But a couple of years ago the legislature at Albany
passed a bill to legalize open betting and to absolve the
race track owners. The New York Tribune of Sunday,
April 22 of that year describes on its front page the
opening of the Jamaica, Long Island race track on the

day before, under the headline, "20,000 Cash Laden Fans Battle to Place Wagers as Jamaica Tracks Open." The article described the bookmakers as being confused by so much money being poked under their noses and that old timers declared they had never seen anything like the struggle that went on under the betting shed ... the jam was so great that women betters had to keep outside. Like a contagious disease this moral letdown has spread over the entire land.

On April 9 the House of Representatives passed a bill to legalize race-track gambling in the District of Columbia, and up to 1,934 bills of similar character had been introduced into 32 states.

There had been introduced into Congress by a member from the State of New Jersey a bill to establish a Federal Lottery with a Grand Prize of $125,000.

Indeed, the day is upon us when we have a "National Conference on Legalizing Lotteries", with one of the prominent ladies of the land as its president, advocating that lotteries should be conducted in the interests of hospitals, charities, and other movements. These "other movements" may consistently be meant to include the Church, for they are telling us that the intelligent church member can well afford to throw his weight in favor of the plan.

Some church members most certainly can, and with painful consistency, for some of the churches, we humiliatingly confess, are even now supporting in part their work by selling chances on a quilt and by other forms of gambling that are no less reprehensible than that which takes place at the racing course or in the gaming room at Bradley's or at Monte Carlo.

The whole nation needs a renewed conscience as to this source of public disgrace and personal degradation, and I think we need it especially in Florida. I have been cautioned against speaking thus plainly because this is a resort. As though this could logically or rightly make any difference. What is wrong anywhere is equally wrong everywhere.

Someone has said that all life is a gamble. Hardly that. But it is a venture. Nothing ventured, nothing gained, we freely admit. The Supreme Court of the state of Kansas, in rendering a decision on Lottery, held that gambling enters in only where "chance is the determining factor." Now, I think that most acceptable - in fact, the only correct answer to the question.

It makes no difference who furnishes the money, or the article representing it. If you take my money or I take yours, or either of us take the money of a third party on the mere outcome of a chance turn of the dice, or of the wheel, or of a card, that is acknowledged to be gambling by the highest authorities both in law and in religion. But if I win that money by an exercise of skill, either physical or mental, run a race for it, or write a poem for it, it cannot, by any propriety whatsoever, be called gambling.

If you want to invest in a share of Woolworth because it pays a good dividend and you believe it is a good stock, I know of no other place to buy it than on the market. And if after a lapse of time that stock becomes more valuable than it was when you first bought it and you sell at a profit, I hardly think it can justly be said that you are a gambler anymore than if you buy a lot in Palm Beach and sell it for more than you paid.

There is, of course, the senseless argument that men always have gambled and always will; why not, therefore, make the best of a thing that can't be helped? Legalize it, license it, and tax it. To argue this is a waste of words. With equal propriety the same thing could be said of every other criminal thing however base and baneful it may be.

There is the age-long argument from the standpoint of Personal Liberty - a man's right to do as he pleases. But a man has no right to do anything that works injury to another man. To contend otherwise is to become sponsor for a type of ethics that is altogether un-manly, un-American, and un-Christian.

There is the argument from the Economic standpoint. We need revenue and here is a way to get it. Here is a new road to prosperity. The repealists told us we could drink our way to it; and now the same class of people are telling us we can gamble our way to it. But where is the nation, the State, or the community that has ever done it? As if a thing that is morally wrong could be economically sound!

AND AGAINST THIS DEADLY VICE I BRING A FIVE-FOLD CHARGE THIS MORNING:

1. Its fundamental concept is at war with honest industry which is always based upon a fair exchange of value. Even a buzzard earns the right to live by cleansing the land of putrefaction, but a gambler, seeing a chance to win something for nothing, loses all love and all incentive for honorable industry. What use to stand behind the counter, or trudge the field in summer sun when at the gaming table he may possibly win at a single stake the salary for a year!

2. It totally unfits a man for honest occupation and profession. It is an unhealthy stimulant. The mind and the imagination are absorbed in the thrill of a possible winning play. The gambling student finds his appointed book work disgusting slavery. The gambling mechanic

has no love for his labor. He is unreliable and untrustworthy.

3. It is a source of dishonesty. Reliable figures, tell us that 90 percent of the defalcations, and theft, and ruin of youth among people who are employed in places of trust is due directly to gambling. The young man will filch money from his father's pocket; the clerk will visit his employer's till; the cashier will empty the banker's vault, and there is no wickedness to which it will not stoop to procure the money to satisfy the merciless appetite that hardens and hurries the thorough-paced gamester on to wretchedness and irreparable ruin.

4. It is a gross violation of the Second Great Commandment to "Love your neighbor as yourself." The gambler to enrich himself is willing to make another man poor. Over 90 percent of those who gamble are losers. If you want to know how Pari mutual race courses, with or without a totalizator, are manipulated, read in "Real America", 'You Can't Beat 'em", by Frank Menke.

Herbert Spencer has well said, "The happiness of the winner involves the misery of the loser." Monte Carlo is famous as a health resort but infamous as a legalized gambling place, and here, we are told, suicides by those who have lost at the gaming tables average at least one a week.

5. It is a violation of a sacred trust. A man doesn't really own anything. What he has has been given him as a sacred trust from God for holy and honorable purposes, and he has no more right to gamble with it than has a trustee a right to gamble with funds entrusted to him for the care of orphans and the aged.

6. Finally, it is a sin in itself - per se. If two men in a duel agree to shoot at each other until one or the

other drops dead, does that make the successful shoot-er any the less a murderer. And if two men agree to take each other's money by the turn of a coin, or any other method where "chance is the determining factor", does that make the winner any less guilty of securing money by the immoral method of taking something for noth-ing?

Perhaps it would be well to stop talking about the evil consequences of this thing and "look squarely", as another man has said, "at the evil face and heart of the thing itself." No matter whether a man "goes in with his eyes open", no matter whether he can afford to lose or not, no matter whether the amount be large or small, the thing itself is immoral, and all right-thinking people have always considered it so, and no amount of gilding or sophistry, or legalizing the thing can make it a virtue.

Stand up, Gambler, and hear your sentence. Your own manhood you are consuming in the fires of a cor-rupt and wicked passion! The finer sensibilities of your nature and all the higher aspirations of your soul you are stifling in the all-absorbing excitement of the game, and your honor, your virtue, your fidelity, your magna-nimity you are trading for the love of winning gold! You are taking from society that for which you are render-ing no service in return, and in your own willingness to lose to another you are violating a sacred trust that came to you from Almighty God!

This may not be true of you, but it is true of thou-sands of other gamblers - like ogres from the under-world they have entered the home of their early love, snatched the bloom from the cheek of a devoted wife, the laughter from the lips and the crust from the hand of their innocent offspring, and left them bowed in unutterable suffering and sorrow as ghastly memorials of a gambler's malignant meanness.

In the room of a New York hotel the chambermaid found the dead body of a young man, and by his side she found a bit of paper on which he had scrawled his last will and testament:

"I leave to society a bad example. I leave to my father and my mother all the sorrow they can possibly bear in their old age. I leave to my friends the memory of a misspent life. I leave to my wife a broken heart, and to my children the name of a gambler and a suicide. I leave to God a lost soul."

I say again, these things, in some particulars, may not be true of you now and may never be - I swing a red light before you to tell you of the danger that lies in the way. The road is down-grade, and the momentum increased as you go. You are no stronger than tens of thousands of others who have been undone by this treacherous enticement, and "self-condemned, have slidden down into eternal night." '

Dr. Biederwolf obviously found no difficulty speaking freely to his congregants, as was the precept set down years before by Henry Flagler. The evangelist gave his last sermon February 6, 1939 and the subject was "Wedding in the Sky." The closing words were prophetic, "I want you to know that Jesus has planned a wedding in the Sky, and I am bringing to you an invitation to meet me over yonder." He suffered a stroke several days later.

Dr. Biederwolf's health had failed in the fall of the previous year and he was not always capable of conducting the Sunday service, relying on such ministers as Dr. Frances M. Fox, Dr. J. P. Muntz and Dr. N. E. Davis. Following the stroke until his passing on Labor Day at Monticello, he was at the Presbyterian Hospital in Chicago and at his home where he had the tender ministrations of Mrs. Biederwolf and a nurse. Perhaps his final weeks were comforted by his love of beautiful flowers and the rare stones that often were used to illustrate his sermons. He was buried at the home cemetery at Monticello after the funeral service at the Presbyterian Church. He had found his peace while the world was going to war.

In 1939, to a grieving Chapel, came Dr. Joseph E. Vance, a good friend of Dr. Howard Lee. From Detroit, Michigan, the man of "eloquence", would preach for two seasons to a large number of worshipers who greatly enjoyed his services. It was prior to America's direct involvement in the World War and the congregation had not yet felt the utterly horrific raid on Pearl Harbor. Dr. Vance had retired from an unusually outstanding pastorate of thirty years at the First Presbyterian Church in Detroit where his reputation was as an eminent and a

Reverend Joseph A. Vance

versatile pastor and an administrator with a "great sense of humor."

There were other ministers who spoke in the Chapel during this period of transition and Dr. John Edward Charlton was one. Adam Sarver was also present and involved in the Chapel, aware of the needs that were ongoing during the three-month season and during a period of growing concern for our nation and the world at war.

It was then, to Dr. John Edward Charlton, English-born Methodist from Morristown, New Jersey, that the Chapel called in the spring of 1941 to become pastor in December of that year. Little did anyone know at the time what December 7th would hold.

Reverend John E. Charlton

WAR YEARS AND DR. CHARLTON

The years of World War II were difficult for most everyone in the nation and the Chapel suffered as well. However, it had its role to play. Gas rationing and travel restrictions took the tourist business from Palm Beach and the Island geared for the widening ripples of war.

Blackout curtains became mandatory and even automobile headlights had to be taped. The Breakers Hotel was taken over by the government and named Ream Hospital, designed to receive war injured. The Biltmore Hotel was converted to a training center for the 'Spars' (women's unit of the Coast Guard) and later as a convalescent hospital for the Navy, providing 1,500 beds.

Young James Arnold was nineteen when he received a scholarship to Georgia Institute of Technology and then was commissioned by the Navy and shipped to the Pacific. Young Marshall McDonald went to fight in the European Theatre of Operation leaving his family behind to wait and wonder and pray each day for an end to the conflict and the safe return of their son. There were many prayers in those days for sons and daughters, brothers and sisters and even fathers and mothers, called to serve both at home and abroad. And the Poinciana Chapel became the place of solace on a Sunday morning for military people as well as families of service personnel. Uniforms became prevalent as people from all over the country came to man the various military installations in the area.

Marjorie Whittemore recalls how it was back then. Daughter of William G. Welsh, she journeyed with the family to Boca Raton before the war and stayed at the Boca Raton Club. Marjorie's daughter, Jeanne, later Mrs. David Reese, was a newborn when they came in September of 1938 after the 'storm', the worst natural disaster to hit the United States, wreaked havoc on the Welsh home on the Massachusetts Cape. During the war they came south by train and Marjorie remembers, "every once in a while we'd get enough gasoline together and hire a car to drive to Palm Beach to see what was going on with the stock market and also to visit a dear family friend, Dr. Sam Lindsay. The trip up A1A was tough — just jungle in those days." When the Boca Club was converted to a nursing home, the Welshes changed their winter locale to Palm Beach.

A significant portion of the municipal airport in West Palm Beach, named Morrison Field, was equipped by the government to serve the Army Air Corps, precursor to the Air Force, and would see over six thousand planes and forty-five thousand pilots processed before wars end.

There were sightings of freighters with smoke billowing from hulls not far offshore and rumors of bloated bodies found floating and of German U-boats menacing the waters close by. David Thompson, who in later years made the Chapel his home church, came to the Palm Beach area in 1925. Raised in West Palm, he performed as altar boy at both St. Ann's and St. Edwards and after graduating from Palm Beach High served with the Civil Air Patrol, flying surveillance along the coast and also took duty as radio man in the shack at Lantana Airport. David witnessed first-hand Marshall Rinker's rage, also as a member of the Patrol, after 'Doc' and Tommy Manning, while flying in the Cape Canaveral area, spotted a German sub stuck on a sandbar. "They telephoned for help but by the time an old Sikorsky amphibian was deployed from the Banana River Naval Air Station the sub was long gone and our observers were furious in their inability to do more than look down upon the struggling sub spewing sand in the air in its attempt to gain escape. Soon after, the small Stinson planes used in the CAP were armed by the Air Corps with bombs and depth charges."

The winds of war blew perilously close to the southeast coast and to Palm Beach. As more evidence of enemy activity was seen, some of the citizenry questioned the local newspapers asking why there were not written reports and a published reply gave answer: "We know what's happening but we're not allowed to write about it!"

It was, then, in 1941 when Dr. John Edward Charlton came to Palm Beach and to a declining congregation and diminished collection, not unlike every other church in the area.

An article from the **Palm Beach Daily News** reports Dr. Charlton's acceptance of the call:

"NEW POINCIANA PASTOR NAMED...

The Rev. John E. Charlton, DD, pastor of the First Methodist Church, of Morristown, New Jersey, has been called to Royal Poinciana Chapel, by the unanimous action of the board of trustees, it was announced Thursday. Dr. Charlton has accepted the call and is to begin his new duties with the opening of next season in December.

Dr. Charlton has been heard twice in the Poinciana pulpit this winter and has made many friends in Palm

Beach. He will be the first regular pastor since the death of Dr. William E. Biederwolf in the summer of 1939.

Letter of Appreciation

A letter of appreciation has been sent by the board to Dr. Joseph A. Vance, pastor emeritus of the First Presbyterian Church, Detroit, who has served as minister-in-charge during the last two seasons, carrying out the pastoral duties and preaching except when visiting ministers were in the pulpit.

A. H. Sarver has been elected president of the board; Henry H. Windsor, Jr., secretary; James Y. Arnold, treasurer; Mrs. Henry H. Windsor, Jr., chairman of the music committee.

The Chapel will remain open through Easter Sunday with Dr. Vance in the pulpit."

Dr. Charlton took the pulpit as "famous preacher and lecturer in the northeast." He proved a very genial man, very friendly, and helped by an able wife. Muriel Catuna remembered Dr. Charlton from her days attending the Methodist Church in Maplewood where she also knew Irma McCall as a fellow grade school student. Muriel spoke fondly of Dr. Charlton crediting him with preaching a wonderfully inspiring children's sermon before the young people left the sanctuary for Sunday school. "He was keen to speak to the hearts of the children and always included humor along with a serious message."

During Dr. Charlton's ministry at the Chapel a four page bulletin was issued. It held a photograph on the front page showing the Chapel, facing north, with a path of gravel in front, and the title:

THE ROYAL POINCIANA CHAPEL

Palm Beach, Florida

John Edward Charlton, Ph. D. Minister

SUNDAY MORNING SERVICE

11 O'CLOCK

On the inside: THE STORY OF ROYAL POINCIANA CHAPEL

"... For many years the Chapel was the only place of worship on the Palm Beach Island and during the time before the erection of the beautiful Saint Edwards Roman Catholic Church the Catholic Altar was erected in the Chapel and the Mass said by a Priest from West Palm Beach each Sunday afternoon. That spirit of Christian fellowship has always been cherished by the ministers who served here.

...In the spring of 1941 the Trustees extended a call to The Reverend John Edward Charlton, Ph. D., the present minister, who assumed the pastorate December first of that year. Dr. Charlton had had an extended ministry in New England after which he served two churches in New Jersey for over twenty years. One notable pastorate being for nineteen years.

... The Trustees are incorporated and are competent to hold in trust the funds and property of the Chapel. The building and grounds are owned and donated for religious worship by the Florida East Coast Hotel Company, which company heartily and generously cooperates with the Trustees in their task of offering to the public a beautiful uplifting and devoutly worshipful service.

... The Chapel congregations are composed of people from all over the United States and Canada. People from Maine and from the state of Washington have been reported at the same service; moreover they are made up of people in a great variety of walks of life and of every denomination.

The Chapel pulpit is known nationwide and the Minister and Trustees seek to render a service which will cultivate in every attendant a clearer sense of the presence of God and a greater desire to do each his part in establishing The Kingdom of God on the earth."

The bulletin makes no mention of the music program but, as directed by Henry Flagler, music at the Chapel continued to be of the finest quality, with few exceptions. While Mr. Flagler lived, Russell Joy was the favorite organist first at the Poinciana Hotel and then at Whitehall and also at the little Chapel. From 1915 to 1922 Miss Hazel R. Bookwalter was organist and pianist and Director of Music. Another organist during that period of time was a Mr. McQuarie and an ensemble of instruments assisted in the music offerings. It was also during Dr. Ward's ministry between 1923 and 1928 that Miss Effie Doe and her mother were organists. According to Arthur D. DeMott's A BRIEF HISTORY OF THE ROYAL POINCIANA CHAPEL, "Miss Doe, an operatic singer, often sang. In 1929 to 1930 a Mr. Zehm was Director and Organist and Mr. and Mrs. George Dunstan, Miss Kluber and Mr. Clegg were among the singers and Mrs. Louise Hunter Windsor was soloist on occasion. Mr. Harry Roe Shelly was also organist from time to time."

The same history credits Dr. Ward with organizing the Sunday school which continued after his decease. There were several classes under the direction of Mrs. Louis Daus, taught by Mrs. A. F. Huston, Mrs. John Kirkton, Mrs. Clifford Savage, Allen Weatherby and Mrs. S. M. Arnold. Mrs. William Harding was listed as Secretary and Rev. William Campbell was Associate Pastor.

DeMott's history confirms that the Chapel was supported by the free will offerings of the people and, "Now comes a new chapter in the history of the Chapel through the securing of a Manse for the Minister. This will add another important link in the service of the Chapel."

According to the history, during Dr. Biederwolf's ministrations, "the Director of Music and Organist was Mrs. Irma Blake Emerson who continued faithfully in that role for eighteen years never missing a service. The quartets which sang during those many years included noted singers and musicians among them: John Charles Thomas, Mrs. Louise Hunter Windsor, Mrs. Louise Homer, of operatic fame, Mrs. Grant and others. Occasionally accompaniment to the service was provided by the ensemble from The Breakers Orchestra, by Mr. Miller and Mr. Yates and other musicians ... all providing many moments of spiritual inspirations.

The Chapel was under the management of the Board of Trustees working in cooperation with the East Coast Hotel Company. Mr. Wm. E. Brode was Chairman for many years, and Mr. Gurnee Munn and George Neuman were treasurers and officials. Mr. A. Sarver was chairman, Frank Reinicke, secretary, J. E. Arnold, treasurer. Milton Fuller, Head Usher, was in charge of flowers which were furnished by The Breakers Gardens under the management of Mr. Lee, Custodian."

Dr. Charlton had served the Chapel through the war years. He had ministered to the needs of loved ones at home and had witnessed the joyful return of many brave heroes as well as the maimed and wounded of spirit and body. During a time of great exuberance and renewal, shocking news came with the sudden illness of the minister during the lenten season of 1947. Dr. Charlton was unable to continue his work and died on the Thursday evening before Palm Sunday by a stroke of apoplexy. His passing was a great shock to all the people in the Palm Beaches by whom he was dearly loved, as well as by hosts of friends in other parts of the country.

The minister, born in Leeds, England in 1879 and nine years old when he came to America, was survived by his wife, who at the time was in residence at the Lotus Cottage adjacent to the Chapel. He left three daughters, Mrs. Grace Button of Maplewood, New Jersey, Mrs. Dorothy Van Leeuwen of Rockport, New York and Miss Ruth Charlton of Madison, New Jersey.

A *Palm Beach Daily News* article dated March 29, 1947 gives details of the funeral arrangements :

> "Funeral services for Dr. John Edward Charlton, pastor of The Royal Poinciana Chapel, who died unex-

pectedly Thursday night, will be held at the Lotus Cottage, on the Poinciana grounds ... Dr. N. E. Davis, who conducted the services last Sunday at the Chapel, will officiate.

Dr. Charlton apparently was in good health until suffering a fatal stroke Thursday evening. The body will be sent to Maplewood, N.J., for further services and burial."

According to Mr. Alfred DeMott's history of the Chapel, Dr. Davis occupied the pulpit the Sundays preceding Dr. Charlton's death and on Easter Day following. Dr. Davis introduced Dr.

Dr. Thomas S. Brock

Thomas S. Brock of Lake Worth as the preacher for the Easter sermon. Dr. Brock had been minister of St. Pauls Church at Atlantic City for more than twenty years, and a scholar of keen ability, lecturer at Temple University in Philadelphia and for seven years had been minister of Calvary Methodist Church at Lake Worth. The Board of Trustees of the Chapel elected Dr. Brock as the minister for the ensuing year.

It was Dr. Brock who assisted in the supervising of the moving of the Chapel during the summer of 1948 to be ready for services in December. The Chapel was moved across the lawn to the northern boundary of the Whitehall adjacent to Lake Trail.

With a new location and new minister the Chapel was about

to embark upon an era of unprecedented growth and profound change. However, it was not Dr. Brock who would inspire the dynamics.

R.
LINDSAY

Adam Sarver saved the Chapel. Uncle Ad knew Dr. Sam Lindsay of Brookline, Massachusetts and persuaded the famous preacher to take the Chapel as a winter mission.

Samuel Macauley Lindsay, born in Prestwick, Ayrshire, Scotland in 1886, was 21 when he came to America. He graduated from Andover-Newton Theological Seminary in 1913 and later took courses at Harvard and Union Theological Seminary in New York.

He served at Euclid Avenue Baptist Church in Cleveland, Ohio as assistant to Dr. Bustard. He married Eleanor Merk, but tragically lost her after six months from Spanish influenza. While in Cleveland he became associated with John D. Rockefeller, Superintendent of the Sunday School at the Baptist Church and a most influential man not only in Cleveland but in many other parts of the country. The two became great friends, enjoying golf twice a week for several years.

Sam Lindsay came from a long line of avid golfers from his grandfather's day and it is written that Sam "had played golf since he was this high to a whippy cleek." Rockefeller had just learned to play the game when they met and it is portentous that Lindsay would be golfing companion to a man who had been so prominently involved with Henry Flagler.

Dr. Lindsay's next pastorate was the Bellevue Baptist Church in Pittsburgh where he met great personalities and wonderful preachers from whom he learned a great deal. When he accepted the call from the Hanson Place Baptist Church in Brooklyn, New York, he again found great inspirational preachers in a community and a church of affluence where he expanded the congregation from a few hundred to a few thousand. The **Brooklyn Eagle** published one of his sermons each month.

His reputation for articulation and compassion preceded him when he was called by the Baptist Church in Brookline in 1922. He would remain in that pastorate for thirty years. It is in Brookline, Massachusetts where he met and married Nellie Hedlund Brooks and it was in Brookline where the minister and his wife became friendly with the Welshes. Marjorie Whittemore confirms that Dr. Lindsay performed her wedding ceremony in Brookline and that the Welsh family visited the Lindsays often in Lake Placid, New York, where Dr. Lindsay was Chaplain during the summer season. It is in Lake Placid where Dr. Lindsay became acquainted with the Carl Eiser family.

The thirty years in Brookline were spent ministering to thousands upon thousands of friends and worshippers. Dr. Lindsay was accepted and cultivated by a host of celebrities, including Edward Everett Hale, Calvin Coolidge, Robert Frost and H. G. Wells. Wells said of Lindsay, "In his voice there is all the color of the Scottish heather and in his utterances the logic of Scottish philosophers and preachers." He spoke to and with the faculty and students from

Harvard and MIT. He valued the friendships of such dignitaries as Harry Emerson Fosdick, S. Parks Cadman, Norman Vincent Peale and such laymen as Will Durant, Charles W. Eliot, president of Harvard College, and was a personal friend of Dwight D. Eisenhower.

It may never be known just who was most instrumental in inspiring the call but it is to Adam Sarver that credit is given for bringing the retiring minister to the Chapel. His services would be for the winter season and his residence while on the Island would be the manse, a small house at 437 Seaview Avenue, acquired for $18,000.

Carl Eiser reported that when Adam Sarver persuaded Dr. Lindsay to come to the Chapel "it was the quickest turn-around I had ever seen. By the early fifties, they had two services with a packed house, and they were handing out a thousand bulletins a Sunday. They had people stacked out on the lawn."

The Minutes from that time show the vigor of the impact of Sam Lindsay's personality. However, he had to work with the East Coast Hotel (The Breakers) and the manager, Mr. Wannop and Mr. Kenan, the owner, both of whom were on the board of the Chapel. They required that the major center sections of the Chapel be set aside for the guests of the hotel.

There were so many stories associated with the Scot who charmed his audiences and became such a presence on the Island. Adam Sarver enjoyed a wonderful golfing companion. They belonged to the Old Guard Society and, as reported by Peggy Scott, "were cozy as two peas in a pod. They would sit together and laugh and giggle." Mrs. Scott also reports, "I didn't know Dr. Brock but he and Dr. Lindsay arrived at the Sarver home in 1949 to baptize my three young daughters. One of the girls looked up, saw two robed gentlemen performing the ceremony, and asked her mother aloud, 'Are they both Jesuses?'"

Hank McCall wrote his "Whistle Tooting" history of the Chapel and describes Dr. Lindsay as "a fun man to be with, a cheerful optimist. You felt that the Living Christ was right there with him, but it was always with a sense of fun. Jesus was there, but let's have fun." Hank goes on to report, "WEAT radio carried his sermons from Jupiter to Miami, and even the charter boats fishing at sea would tune in to Sam Lindsay's sermons. Dr. Lindsay had an image of what his job was: 'The minister's job is to preach the gospel, keep the pews filled, the bills paid, and to be available every day for those in trouble.' He certainly practiced what he preached and had a marvelous sense of humor. He always prefaced his remarks for raising money with a joke. And he was soon such a popular personality on the Island that raising money was never a problem."

Lois Krueger began attending the Chapel in 1950. She and her husband stayed at "The Everglades Hotel within walking distance of the Chapel." It is there where they became acquainted with the Eisers. Lois relates that Dr. Lindsay was, "a marvelous speaker, his sermons simply wonderful. He was very dedicated to the Chapel and knew everybody in town and everybody knew Dr. Lindsay. He was accustomed to having his own way and he always got his own way. When the board told him he couldn't have five or ten thousand dollars for something he deemed important, he just called up Mrs. Phipps or Mr. Love and they didn't hesitate to write a check." Lois reveres Dr. Lindsay for his honesty, "he had a reputation for being completely honest and straight forward. If he didn't like something you were doing, he just told you." Dr. Lindsay referred to Lois Krueger, with strong Scottish brogue as, "my joyful friend."

Marjorie Whittemore had enjoyed attending the Chapel before the war and she continued to spend winters in Palm Beach. She relates staying in a rented house on Seaview near the Four Arts and the ocean. "Dr. Lindsay lived in the manse close by." "Dr. Lindsay, like Mr. Welsh (her father), was a gentle Scot with a wonderful sense of humor. He always included a humorous story or joke in the middle of his sermon that put everyone in a good humor

... be it a story about people or animals it always charmed his audience." Marjorie credits Dr. Lindsay during the war years with calling on people who suffered tragic losses "due to the war." "His caring and compassion was felt by many." She also witnessed the minister's life in the manse, "Dr. and Mrs. Lindsay lived in a small house on Seaview close to where we rented from Mr. and Mrs. Behr. Dr. Lindsay was not well paid by the Chapel." Marjorie also relates, "Father rented the Sea Gull Cottage for ten years until 1967." Located on the ocean and just north of The Breakers Hotel, "the cottage was not luxurious for the times. It did have an enormous kitchen with restaurant-sized stove and refrigerator, a laundry room and many bedrooms but not too many baths. The furnishings left a lot to be desired and the only heat source was a pot-bellied stove in the middle of the living room."

Marjorie recalls that when they first attended the Chapel, "the building faced north on the property in front of the Whitehall and many of the congregants sat on chairs on the lawn. That was a good arrangement when the weather permitted because it was a better place with a young child."

The Welsh family hosted the Lindsays in their home in Falmouth "many, many times and we loved Sam as dearly as we loved Nell." Marjorie remembers, "it was amusing to watch and listen as Sam would sweetly admonish or correct Nell in their conversations from time to time ... but it wasn't ever done with a raised voice ... and she usually needed to be corrected!"

Dr. Lindsay was a flirt with the ladies, according to Hank McCall's history of the Chapel, but, "his wife, Nell, kept him on a tight rein." One of the things he would say to the ladies was poetic:

"As is the mint sauce to the lamb
As is the fried egg to the ham
As is the possum to the yam
Are you to me.
Like pork without the applesauce
Or a hot cross bun without a cross

Without you, love
A total loss my life would be."

His wife apparently had no say in the minister's gastronomic habits. Each evening he enjoyed two neat scotches and began each day at Benny's with a hearty repast. Apparently he had little concern about cholesterol. He ordered two eggs up, with a pat of butter on each, four or five rashers of bacon and a pile of grits with a pool of melted butter swimming in the center. He enjoyed two pieces of white toast, slathered with butter and jelly and four or five cups of coffee generously dolloped with cream and sugar. Hank and Irma McCall entertained the Lindsays at dinner and remember that he enjoyed the meat and potatoes but never cared for vegetables. And he "smoked cigars up until ten years before he died at ninety-nine and a half."

"He was a terrible driver - tough on his automobiles. He'd get busy talking and telling jokes and, wham!; he'd have a fender-bender. There was always a crowd around Dr. Lindsay to hear the latest stories. He was known to preface each telling with, 'mind you, we are not gossiping, merely reporting.' He loved to say, 'The best days of the Chapel are ahead of us, not behind us.' 'Image of magnificence' was used when he described his fellow man and he often advised, 'Keep riding your bicycle until you fall off.' In speaking of God's love, 'Instant forgiveness - constant love.'"

He gave current event lectures every Friday afternoon to four hundred attendees and he wrote a column for the **Shiny Sheet**. One was titled "The True History of Golf" and excerpts are colorful in revealing Dr. Lindsay's view of the game:

"Golf was first played in Scotland by the Romans.

They played in kilts and planted heather on the hillside to mark boundary lines.

They played the bagpipes to scare off the fighting Scots.

The game of golf was first commercialized at St. Andrews which is a 'Royal and Ancient Burough.'

Soon there was a golf course in every cow pasture and 'Cow Pasture Pool' was played by every Scot who had kilts.

They used but one club. It was a wood spoon with a whippy shaft. Most of the spoons are still in existence. The Scots never give away anything except tips on the races.

While the men played golf the women knitted socks and made golf balls. They were made of soft leather filled with feathers. A good putting ball was filled with hen feathers so to keep it on the ground. A good driving ball was filled with pigeon feathers so that it would fly. When rubber was discovered, it was an answer to a Scotchman's prayer for a ball that would last a life-time. The Gutta Percha ball was as near to being everlasting as anything in existence. It was first used in 1849. When a ball was lost it was searched for until found. When it became square instead of round it was remolded on the kitchen fire. The Gutta Percha ball died when Haskell invented the rubber cored ball in the United States.

Iron clubs were first used in Prestwick where the second oldest club is located. We don't know who made the first cleek, but the first MASHIE was made by Old Johnnie Gray.

The game was brought to America by the Scots.

They also brought Scotch Haggis.

The average American took to golf like a duck to water but only those who had a Ph.D. and Phi Beta Kappa key appreciate "haggis." It is oatmeal and lard which has had a college education.

The game appealed to Americans as a post graduate course in arithmetic. Most men who played it developed a genius for subtraction but were slow in acquiring the art of addition.

It also appealed to the men as an escape mecha-
nism. It enabled men to escape from their wives and to
escape from their brokers when margin calls were on
the way. Then the women took it up and golf is now fast
becoming a family affair and the Country Club an
annex to the living room. We used to play golf with four
clubs: a driver, cleek, mashie and putter. Now a golfer
carries so many clubs that he needs a truck instead of
a caddie.

We are developing the best politicians in the world
and the best golfers on earth. We have developed Walter
Travis, Francis Ouimet, Bobby Jones, Lawson Little,
President Eisenhower, and members of the Old Guard.

Some get a lot of fun out of the game, others only
get sales prospects, corns and Athletes Foot."

Hank McCall remembers that Dr. Lindsay played golf in an
everyday business suit and that he was a two or three handicapper.
Along with Adam Sarver, he enjoyed the game enormously and
enjoyed the fellowship of the Old Guard Society members. He also
belonged to the Everglades Club and he attracted businessmen of
great ability and made slaves of them. "They worked their heads off
for Dr. Lindsay." The good doctor was a very practical man, according to Hank, "and this is the characteristic of every preacher we
have had here at the Chapel. They were very practical people. They
were businessmen. They ran the church within their budgets. They
did not create debts."

In 1957 the Trustees of the Chapel honored Adam Sarver at
their annual meeting. Considered one of the old residents of Palm
Beach, he served as Chairman of the Trustees for eighteen consec-
utive years from 1939. He had held the Chapel together during the
difficult years prior to and during the war. He had a strong affection
for Butler, Pennsylvania where hospitals, churches and welfare
institutions were strengthened by his benevolence. He enjoyed the

game of golf and shot an 88 on his eighty-eighth birthday. On his ninetieth, after eating lunch with family and friends, he went out and demonstrated on the Palm Beach Golf Course that he could still play. His score for nine holes was 46. He loved Sam Lindsay as a man, as his minister and dear friend and as fellow golfer.

Adam Sarver President of Board 1939 - 1957

When he died in 1960, a portrait of Uncle Ad hung inside the north entrance of the Chapel. The original portrait by Charles von Hausen located in the Little Chapel had been restored by Mignon Gardner. Hank McCall wrote a biographical sketch of Mr. Sarver so that, "we might better understand his contribution to the continuance of The Royal Poinciana Chapel." The bio was headed "OLD GUARDIAN, 1930-1960 Adam Sarver." Uncle Ad was gone but his legacy lives on.

The Sunday bulletins printed during Dr. Lindsay's pastorate are a wonderful resource and most insightful. In 1957 they held a photograph of the Chapel with dirt path in front and the Whitehall mansion to the right and the heading: The Royal Poinciana Chapel, Flagler Memorial, Cocoanut Row and Whitehall Way, Palm Beach, Florida. At the bottom of the front cover: Rev. Samuel M. Lindsay, D.D., Minister, and beneath: 437 Seaview Avenue, Palm Beach,

Chapel Telephone: TEMPLE 2-2521.

It is presumed that when one called the Chapel at TEMPLE 2-2521, the telephone was answered by Dr. Lindsay's secretary, Bert Hunt. When Dr. Lindsay first came to the Chapel, according to Marilyn Polete, he acted as his own secretary. When the workload required an assistant, a young woman named "Bert Hunt" was hired part-time. Dr. Lindsay later referred to her as "a character - a bit of a Bohemian." She was reputed to dress in rather avant garde attire and rode around the Island in a golf cart. When she decided that an area in the Chapel set aside as an office, with couch and a small refrigerator, would be ideal for her 'home', she moved in and "lived there" unnoticed for some time. In later years when Bert developed cancer and was practically bed-ridden, living in a small cottage on Cocoanut Row just south of Royal Palm Way, Dr. Lindsay visited her and took along "a Bible and a bottle of booze."

The bulletins on which Bert Hunt labored reveal some of the thoughts and direction of Dr. Lindsay's services.

Sunday, January 27, 1957 gives the Order for the 9:15 A.M. Services. A Cello and Organ Prelude was followed by "Holy, Holy, Holy" and the Rachmanioff Anthem - "Blessing and Glory." The Chapel Quartette included Arlene Winger, Soprano, Elise Zaro, Alto, Ted Milford, Tenor and Jonathan Koontz, Bass. Organist: Dr. Charleton Bullis and Cellist: Mrs. Henry Yates. The sermon "Psychology and Religion III" preceded the ever-present Doxology and Presentation of Offering. On the inside page:

In Memoriam, FRANK MARION SWANSON, 1895 - 1956

Excerpts from the obituary give historical grounding to early Palm Beach:

"Swanson, of Kissimmee, had graduated from the School of Engineering of the University of Florida in 1917. He was employed as Chief Engineer on the building of the Palm Beach Canal from Lake Okeechobee to Lake Worth. In 1923 he was Engineer in charge of the construction of the Gulf Stream Golf Course and served as first Mayor of Gulf Stream. He worked under Mr. H. E. Bemis of the Florida East Coast Hotel Company as Engineer in charge of the Hotel Company Properties consisting of gardens and grounds and two golf courses at Palm Beach, at Key West and golf courses and gardens and grounds at Miami, St. Augustine and Ormond Beach.

After the burning of the old Breakers in 1925 and the building of the new Breakers, the relocation of some of the buildings required the revamping of some of the holes. During his tenure the greens were changed from sand to turf.

In 1928 he was in charge of the construction of the nine-hole golf course on the Edward F. Hutton estate and in 1929 served as Engineer in charge of the construction of the Seminole Golf Course.

Mr. Swanson served in two wars. In World War I he served as Second Lieutenant, and in World War II he entered as a Captain and was discharged as a Major.

He served as Chief Engineer of Construction and Maintenance for the Florida East Coast Hotel Company and as member of the Zoning Board of the Town of Palm Beach. He served on the Town Council before and again after his military service.

Mr. Swanson was retired on pension February 1, 1956, having had over 31 years' service with the Hotel Company. He passed away on October 25, 1956 at the Veterans Hospital at Coral Gables at the age of 61 years."

The back cover of the bulletin held a report including a brief history of the Chapel:

"Mr. A. H. Sarver of Detroit, Chairman of the

Trustees of the Chapel. The Chapel is entirely dependent for its support upon the free will offerings of those who attend the service. We have no other source of income.

Today we honor Mr. Henry M. Flagler who built The Royal Poinciana Chapel and thank all who have perpetuated its spiritual ministry by their generous gifts."

The bulletin for Sunday, March 17, 1957 lists the diverse religions represented by the Sunday last registration cards:

Baptist 372	Disciples 96
Presbyterian 461	Quaker 18
Methodist 203	Universalist 4
Congregational 176	Unitarian 32
Reformed 98	Brethren 24
Lutheran 159	Unity 12
Episcopalian 163	Christian Science 88
United Church of Canada 99	Roman Catholic 36
Christian 84	Greek Catholic 22
Jewish 52	Moslem 3

A notice included: The Art of Living Together, Friday 4 p.m.

On Friday at four o'clock, Doctor Lindsay will give a lecture on THE FINE ART OF LIVING TOGETHER. This will be an hour of joy and inspiration. The lecture has been delivered more than one thousand times. Roger Babson said, "The best lecture I ever heard." On the back page of the bulletin were philosophical thoughts on war:

War Is Crazy

War Is Cruel

War is Costly

They that take up the sword shall perish by the taxes.

— Cleveland News

Every war ends where it should have begun: by peace.

— Abbe Barthelemy

Standing armies have created ten wars where they have prevented one. — Thomas Jefferson

The great duty of our generation is to put a stop to man-killing as the great work of Lincoln's generation was to put a stop to man-selling.　　— Carnegie

If Christians were only to admit ... that a Christian cannot be a murderer, there would then be no soldiers..
　　— Tolstoy

By killing in mutual wars the best physically developed men, we must become more and more degenerate.
　　— Tolstoy

A great war leaves the country with three armies - an army of cripples, an army of mourners, and an army of thieves.　　— German Proverb

For him who takes the sword, the sword is always in readiness.　　**— The Outlook**

The most hoary-headed lie which ever tormented the human race is the old, worn-out lie — proved false a thousand times — that great armies and great navies are assurances of peace.　— Senator William E. Borah

It makes no difference what leagues or associations nations may form. If nations arm against each other for war, war will ensue in the end. — David Lloyd George

Clubs and bows and arrows do not solve problems. They simply clean the slate.
　　— Bishop Edward L. Parsons

Its heroisms are but the glancing sunlight on a sea of blood and tears.　　— Harry E. Fosdick

One of the most important tasks for our generation is to develop a social, ethical and economic basis upon which nations can live together in peace.
　　— S. M. Lindsay

The bulletin dated Sunday, April 7, 1957 includes a prayer:

Lord, make me dream of all I hope to see
In the new world of peace that soon will be,
Dream of the good that must be shared by all,

An equal chance in life for great and small.

Lord, make me strong to work the whole day through
That I may help my dreaming to come true,
Putting aside all thought of my own gain,
Easing the load of poverty and pain.

Lord, let me pray that in true brotherhood
We may strive only for each other's good.
Dreams, work and prayer all patterns in Thy plan
Of selfless happiness and peace for man.

— Beatrice Gibbs

Under the heading ANNUAL MEETING 1957 there is an interesting joining of names held on one page of the bulletin:

"At the Annual Meeting of the Trustees, Mr. E. H. Taylor was elected Chairman for the coming year. Mr. Russell P. Taber was elected a Trustee. Mr. Alvin W. Boettcher was elected Secretary. Mr. J. Y. Arnold was re-elected Treasurer. The meeting was characterized by understanding, harmony and enthusiasm." And beneath the notice was listed:

"THE TWELVE DISCIPLES

Simon, Peter, Thomas, Andrew, his brother Matthew James, son of Zebedee James, son of Alpheus, John, son of Zebedee, Thaddeus, Philip, Simon, the Zealot Bartholomew, Judas"

And beneath that:

CHAPEL USHERS

James Y. Arnold	Herman Fleer	Alvin W. Boettcher
Milton A. Fuller	George W. Coleman	Aubrey G. Gilmore
Charles W. Collins	Algot M. Johnson	Francis C. Dittrich
Charles J. Kuntz	William H. Dyer	Carl Reese
Carl H. Eiser	Carl B. Tuttle	Homer Evilsizor
		J. Bruce Wallace"

116

According to the bulletin for Easter:

Sunday April 21, 1957 Elsa Moegle played the Harp Offertory: "Au Rouet" by Zabel and "One Early Easter Morning" by Maryott. Also included were three writings:

"YOUTH

Youth is not a time of life ... it is a state of mind. It is not a matter of ripe cheeks, red lips, and supple knees ... it is a temper of the will, a quality of the imagination, a vigor of the emotions. It is the freshness of the deep springs of life.

Youth means a temperamental predominance of courage over timidity, of the appetite for adventure over the love of ease. This often exists in a man of fifty more than in a boy of twenty.

Nobody grows old by merely living a number of years. People grow old only by deserting their ideals. Years wrinkle the skin but to give up your enthusiasm wrinkles the soul. Worry, doubt, self-distrust, fear and despair ... these are the long, long years that bow the heart and turn the greening spirit back to dust.

Whether sixty or sixteen, there is in every human being's heart the lure of wonder, the sweet amazement at the stars and at starlike things and thoughts, the undaunted challenge of events, the unfailing, childlike appetite for what next, and the joy of the game of living. You are as young as your faith, as old as your doubt; as young as your self-confidence, as old as your fear; as young as your hope, as old as your despair.

In the central place of your heart is an evergreen tree . . . its name is Love. So long as it flourishes you are young. When it dies you are old. In the central place of your heart is a wireless station. So long as it receives messages of beauty, hope, cheer, grandeur, courage and power from God and from your fellow men, so long are

117

you young." And then a writing:

"80 YEARS OLD. When John Quincy Adams was 80 years old a friend met him in Boston and said: 'How is John Quincy Adams?' He replied: 'John Quincy Adams himself is very well, thank you, but the house he lives in is dilapidated. It is tottering on its foundation. The walls are badly shattered and the roof is worn. The building trembles, and I think John Quincy Adams will have to move out before long. But he himself is very well.'"

A lady in the congregation read this and wrote the following letter to the Minister:

"'The house I live in is 82 years old. Considering its age, it is in good repair, though it does not look as good as it did 50 years ago. I have neglected to keep it painted as so many women of this generation do. To tell the truth, I have been spending my time in interior decorating.'

'The windows I look out of are fairly clean, and I am glad to tell you I have a reliable tenant in the upper story.'"

At the bottom of the third page of the bulletin was a notice:

"Sunday, April 28, 1957, 11 a.m., Next Sunday there will be but one service. It will begin at eleven o'clock. The service will be broadcast from 11:30 to 12 over Station WEAT."

On the back page of the bulletin was a Dr. Lindsay essay:

"THE UNTROUBLED HEART

Let not your heart be troubled

1. Let not your heart be troubled about DEMOCRACY.

It suits us.

118

Our form of government fits our emotional and psychological life.

It confers the greatest possible benefits on the largest number of people. It is flexible and can be adjusted to changing conditions.

It has conferred upon us the maximum degree of liberty in speech, press, finance, conscience, and religion.

The average citizen is sufficiently intelligent to know that he is better off in a democracy than he could possibly be under any other existing form of government.

We are not going to have a bloody revolution in the United States.

We are not going communistic.

Don't let them scare you!

It can't happen here!

2. Let not your heart be troubled about CIVILIZATION.

There are many bad people in the world, but there are more good people than bad people.

The good people outnumber the bad people.

There is a constant fight going on between the higher and the lower, and the higher is winning.

God is on the side of goodness, and although evil is mighty, God is Almighty.

Don't let them scare you!

Civilization is not bound for the scrap heap of the universe.

The progress of humanity is upward and onward forever!

3. Let not your heart be troubled about DEATH.

Death is not an accident to life; it is but an incident in life.

Your body is just an automobile in which you travel around.

You will continue to live after you discard your body.

You are an immortal soul that lives in a body.

Don't let them scare you about death.

Death is an old door in a garden wall.

On the other side of the wall is life, and not death.

'For God so loved the world, that He gave His only begotten Son, that whosoever believeth in Him should not perish, but have everlasting life.'

— S. M. Lindsay"

Marjorie Whittemore gives testimony to the compassion of Dr. Lindsay. "When Mr. Welsh died in January of 1964, the family was in Falmouth and realistically did not expect Dr. Lindsay to attend the funeral of his dear friend due to the fact that Dr. Lindsay was in Palm Beach at the time. When the call was placed to Dr. Lindsay informing of the death of Mr. Welsh, the family expressed, 'It is a pity that you cannot be here for the funeral because Mr. Welsh would want you more than anyone in the world to be here.' Dr. Lindsay's reply was without hesitation, 'I'll be there!' The wonderful minister, in his eighties at the time, got on a plane to Boston where he was met by family members and a terrible blizzard. The weather could not have been worse. We had booked a room at the Ritz but Dr. Lindsay was adamant that he preferred to be with the family members on that occasion just as he had, along with Nell, many times before as they made their yearly trip to Lake Placid."

There were many wonderful facets to the man. His sense of people, his compassionate, keen awareness and his humor, always in tact, drew people to him and entertained immeasurably. A story that he loved to relate had him walking through the Boston Commons on a raw, rainy day. There he saw a forlorn, pathetic little man seated, drenched from the rain, water dripping from his hat, his coat collar turned up. Dr. Lindsay approached, put a ten dollar bill in the man's lap and spoke with compassion, "Never despair!" Dr. Lindsay continued on his way. Two days later, on a dazzling, blue-sky day, Dr. Lindsay was again walking through the Commons when he felt a tug at his sleeve and looked down to see the same wretched little man, who handed him a hundred dollars - "'Never Despair' came in at Aqueduct ... hit it on the nose, Dr. Lindsay ... on the nose!'"

Dr. Lindsay had a devoted parishioner named Walter Johnson who sat, faithfully, in the third row directly on the aisle Sunday after Sunday. It is reported by Hank McCall that one day "Walter went calling on Dr. Lindsay, saying 'Dr. Lindsay, I've got ten thousand dollars ... and there's a horse running down at Hialeah named Walter's Boy ... and I want to put the whole ten thousand dollars on him to win. Would you please bless me and bless my bet?'

Dr. Lindsay, minister as well as frugal Scotsman, was horrified by the idea and proceeded to tell Walter all about the evils of gambling and even talked him out of making the bet. The following Sunday Walter Johnson was not present in 'his' seat. The next Sunday the seat remained vacant - glaringly so. Finally, the minister's curiosity got the better of him and he went by to see Walter. Dr. Lindsay questioned, 'What's the matter with ye? Have ye been ill?' 'No,' was the curt answer, 'I'm not going to your church anymore! If I'd put that ten thousand on Walter's Boy I'd have seventy thousand dollars.' From that time forward Walter Johnson attended Sunday service at Bethesda."

Hank and Irma McCall came to Palm Beach in 1952 from Greensboro, North Carolina where they attended the downtown First Presbyterian Church. Hank was a salesman working in the plumbing supply business and says he was poor and struggling at the time. He was in business with Clarence Coston, who was killed in an airplane accident. In 1964, Hank suffered serious business reversals, taking on a contract that caused him to lose everything. He was broke and, needless to say, it was an extremely stressful time for Hank and Irma. Hank's parents had been attending the

Chapel, as fans of Dr. Lindsay, and they persuaded Hank to attend with them. It took Hank from his Sunday fishing trips and Irma away from Memorial Presbyterian where they attended with their children. The McCalls became enthralled with Dr. Lindsay's sermons, receiving spiritual strength and inspiration through the financial crisis as well as the tragic loss of a son. Hank fully credits Dr. Lindsay's cheerful optimism with helping work through and beyond the trauma. Hank and "Irmie" became devotees of both the minister and the Chapel.

One of Hank's favorite sermons by the renowned minister was entitled "The Land of Beginning Again." Another was "Roses Will Bloom Again", a copy of which had been stuck in a drawer for many years and was sent to Hank by Mac Warwick. Hank found it to be as "bright and as fresh as it could be." Another, "Immortality", an Easter Sermon, was given in copy form to Mac Warwick by James Arnold. The frontispiece held two thoughts:

> "Think of stepping on shore
> And finding it Heaven.
> Of taking hold of a hand
> And finding it God's hand.
> Of breathing a new air
> And finding it celestial air.
> Of feeling invigorated
> And finding it immortality.
> Of passing from storm and tempest
> To perfect calm.
> Of waking and knowing
> I am home."

and then, "Francis of Assisi, hoeing his garden, was asked what he would do if he were suddenly to learn that he was to die at sunset that day. He said: 'I would finish hoeing my garden.'" Within the text of the sermon: "A normal person believes in immortality.

> It is as much a part of his psychological make-up as his ears are a part of his physical make-up. He knows his

body is not immortal, but believes 'he' is immortal. He knows his body was built to last for a limited number of years and finally will disintegrate and disappear, but believes his invisible and real self will continue to live after he passes through the experience of death. It was because he believed this that Theodore Roosevelt said: 'I believe death is the greatest experience in life.'

Belief in immortality gives dignity to life and enables us to endure cheerfully the trials which come to all. It saves us from becoming too deeply engrossed in selfish pursuits and gives each of us a higher regard for our neighbors. Belief in immortality is no coward's philosophy, but a wholesome faith which inspired us to be noble and unselfish.

Jesus taught us when we pray to say: 'Our Father who art in Heaven.' Ever since Christ taught us to think of God as our Father, there has been an expanding confidence in immortality. This faith is the concomitant of the Christian conception of God. Those who believe God is their Father and they are His children believe that they will continue to live after they die.

Some day we will lay aside our bodies as we lay aside our winter clothing, but we will continue to live. It takes faith to believe this, but such faith has been one of the outstanding characteristics of the disciples of Christ for twenty centuries.

Recently I visited an old churchyard in Cooperstown, New York, and read a verse of poetry on a tombstone that was almost two hundred years old: 'And when I die, I'll rise on high to meet a smiling God.'

The faith of this early settler ... set the joy bells ringing in my heart. Men who possess this faith live as men prepared to die, and die as men prepared to live.

Dr. Ray Petty of Philadelphia was facing death and

knew it. Writing to a friend, he said: 'I look forward without fear but with the confidence that in the life beyond there will be opportunity for growth and for useful service. When I meet God I will say: What is the next big job you have for me to do?'

I, too, look forward to the future with faith and joyful expectations.   I believe that the road's last turn will be the best, and that when God's servant whom we call 'death' opens the door, I will pass into a better world where God will prepare me to render better service than I have done here in this world."

And on the inside back cover of the sermon, no credit given for authorship:

"Within the maddening maze of things
When tossed by storm and flood
To one fixed trust my spirit clings,
I know that God is good.

And so beside the silent sea
I wait the muffled oar
No harm from Him can come to me
On ocean or on shore.

I know not where his islands lift
Their fronded palms in air,
I only know I cannot drift
Beyond His love and care."

Hank McCall speaks highly of many individuals who have been associated with the Chapel over the years. He praises John Stetson, architect, as someone who was influential as President of the Board of the Chapel. It was John who had Hank ushering within his first year of attendance. Hank moved on to serve as secretary on the board and became deeply committed to the workings of the Chapel. He opines "there was a constant series of outstanding men who served the Chapel." He gives accolades to "Alvin Boettcher, Arthur M. (Bay) Gee and Bill Tell who came later, Carl Eiser was another ... just outstanding men that I greatly admired." Hank explains that most of the men were retired and he was the "young kid."

Dr. Stanley Inman

MORT KAYE STUDIOS, INC.

The bulletin for April 24, 1966 holds a photograph of the Chapel, the Whitehall retouched out and the path in front paved instead of shell rock. There are six steps leading to the front entry and steps on either side leading to doors protected by covered porches - the steps and porches reduced in recent years. Beneath the photograph are listed the names under the heading Ministers:

Rev. Samuel M. Lindsay, D.D.

Rev. Stanley M. Inman, D.D.

Dr. Lindsay was in his eighties when Dr. Stanley Inman was called to be assistant to Dr. Lindsay. However, Dr. Lindsay would never yield the pulpit to the man who was a great Baptist preacher from Los Angeles. Dr. Inman, according to Hank McCall, "would talk at Rotary Club and various civic organizations. He was a marvelous speaker, but the aging Scot would not permit the new man to preach in the pulpit and so Dr. Inman read the Bible and he put all his energy, all his love and his pathos into reading the Scripture. You have never heard such Scripture reading as Dr. Stanley Inman gave here at The Royal Poinciana Chapel."

The bulletin for April 24, 1966 lists Mr. John Stetson as President of Trustees, Mr. Alvin W. Boettcher, Past President, Mr. James Y. Arnold, Past President, Mr. Edmund H. Taylor, Past

President, Mr. Vernon Raedisch, Treasurer, and Mr. C. H. McCall, Secretary. The choir comprised Mrs. Ruth Palmer, Mrs. Evangeline Pugliese, Mr. Ted Milford, Mr. Warren Pylman and at the Organ, Mr. C. Russell Henderson.

John Stetson President of Board 1966 - 1974

MORT KAYE STUDIOS, INC.

On the back cover were inspirational pieces: "WHAT OUR RELIGION SHOULD DO FOR US

1. Give us a satisfactory conception of God.

2. Bring us in personal contact with the living Christ, of whom Paul said: 'I can do all things through Christ, which strengthens me.'

3. Teach us that the Christ way is the best way in the new day.

4. Give us power to overcome sin and strength to live the Christlike life.

5. Give us courage to face reality and strength to perform our duties.

6. Teach us to forgive those who have injured us and to love those we are tempted to hate.

7. Teach us to love the beautiful.

8. Teach us the art of harmonious living.

9. Inspire us to fight the devil and all his works.

10. Lead us to cooperate with others in building Christian ideals into the home, city, nation, and world.

11. Teach us to believe that God will be triumphant over the devil and that war, crime, racism, and ignorance may be banished from the earth.

12. Teach us to believe that death is not an end of life, but the door into the perfect life in a better country."

And another thought on the back page of the bulletin:

"WHAT IS A WILL

A will is a wish - sealed in words; your last word spoken, yet irrevocable; your philosophy of life - made public forever; a cameo of your character - internal and external; your living faith - echoing through the years; a perpetual participation in things you love - and the state assumes responsibility for its implementation; your absentee ballot - a vote for things eternal; your legal resurrection - you being dead, yet speaking!

REMEMBER THE CHAPEL IN YOUR WILL

Some of our friends have already done this and we hope others will do so. We want to perpetuate the work of the Chapel. Remember what Stanley High said: 'The things that I get from my church are not offered anywhere else. And I get along better with those things than without them.'"

Marilyn Polete came to work for Dr. Lindsay in 1966. From Collinsville, Illinois, she and Richard were high school sweethearts. They moved to Florida in 1954. Marilyn was raised a Catholic and Dick was a Methodist but neither had been regular church attendees until she took the position of Secretary, the

Marilyn (Mrs. Richard) Polete

job gained through the Florida State Employment.

Soon after she began working at the Chapel a bulletin was printed with a typo listing Marilyn as "V Mary Polete" and from that time on Dr. Lindsay, who had difficulty pronouncing 'Marilyn', called her "the Virgin Mary." For that reason many still call her Mary and do not realize that her name is Marilyn.

Dr. Lindsay was in his eighties when Marilyn began working at the Chapel and she found quite a different Chapel and a differ-

Left to right: Pres. Dwight Eisenhower, Seward Patterson, Dr. Lindsay

ent Palm Beach back then. "The Chapel was open from November until the end of May when Dr. Lindsay went north to be Summer Chaplain at the Lake Placid Club. During the summer the Chapel was locked, but the key hung on a nail at the front entry for anyone to use." Marilyn picked up the mail and performed all the necessary paper work at her home during the summer hiatus.

"The Chapel didn't have a membership at that time, only attenders who came to the 'Preaching Station.' It was at a time when The Breakers Hotel, open only for season, was more a resi-

dential hotel with regulars coming each season to occupy apartments within the hotel. There were a hundred seats reserved every Sunday for the guests from The Breakers. The attendance was so high that 'funeral chairs' were placed on the front lawn for the overflow with loudspeakers used to convey the sermon to those seated outside."

Many of the wealthy Palm Beachers were regulars and whenever there was

President Richard Nixon

need for financial assistance it was answered readily. Marilyn recalls, "when a new roof was required, Dr. Lindsay stood up on Sunday morning, prefacing his request as he always did before each collection, with a story. Before the week was out he had $26,000 collected for the new roof."

Dr. Lindsay's reputation and influence reached across many boundaries. He was invited on one occasion to preside at the opening session of Congress, offering the Invocation to an auspicious congregation of politicians in Washington. He was a worker, one Marilyn found "to be perfectly happy working seven days a week, and he expected me to do the same."

Marilyn remembers Dr. Lindsay as a "wonderful man, a real individual." She credits the **Shiny Sheet** running a picture on the front page, showing Dr. Lindsay wearing his kilt, and the caption,

"Do you know who this man is? ... he's the friendliest man in Palm Beach."

However, the friendliest man, she discovered, was not a good driver and Marilyn often drove Dr. Lindsay about town. "He had dings in his car that were never accounted for ... One day my car was parked outside the church and Dr. Lindsay ran into it. When I pointed out the fact to him he seemed quite unconcerned asking only that 'I hope it's nae badly hurt!'"

The friendliest man in town spoke to many VIP's over the years. One Easter Sunday Lowell Thomas was in the congregation when Dr. Lindsay preached the sermon on Immortality. Thomas thought so much of the words that he returned for the second service. Richard Nixon came to town to speak at the Round Table meeting held in the Chapel. His motorcade created a huge traffic jam and the Round Table was forbidden henceforth to have afternoon programs at the Chapel.

Robert Schuler also attended service and spoke to a delighted audience at the Chapel. When Dr. Lindsay was to preach a sermon that was advertised in the newspaper entitled, "Is It Fate Or the Will of God?" Oral Roberts was staying at The Breakers along with his son. Dr. Lindsay was alerted and called the TV evangelist, inviting him to speak at the Sunday service. When the invitation was accepted, there was great anticipation on the part of Dr. Lindsay, eager to surprise the congregation. His introduction from the pulpit was augural, "Well, I'm here this morning ... prepared to preach on Fate or the Will of God ... and I want to ask you ... we have Oral Roberts here this morning ... Is It Fate or the Will of God?"

Dr. Lindsay was always welcoming to any guest speakers but never permitted Dr. Inman to preside in the pulpit. Dr. Inman remained in the capacity of Assistant for a couple of years before returning to California. His name, according to Marilyn, "is not listed on the plaque listing the ministers who have served the Chapel."

It was Jean Flagler Matthews, granddaughter of Henry Flagler, who decided the fate of the Chapel. She wanted to put in a garden and lawn on the property leading to the Whitehall Museum from Cocoanut Row. She also wished to have an unobstructed view from Whitehall to The Breakers. The mansion had been sold by Flagler's heirs and served as an elegant hotel residence from 1925 until 1959, when Mrs. Matthews purchased the property and painstakingly acquired as many of the original furnishings as possible. The restored landmark was opened as a museum to the public in 1960. The request for removal of the Flagler Memorial Chapel, The Little White Church by the Trail, was made with five years to accomplish the actual move.

60 COCOANUT ROW

According to a letter and accompanying Designation Report from the Town of Palm Beach Planning, Zoning and Building Department and Landmarks Preservation Commission, dated February 13, 1991, to Royal Poinciana Chapel Trustees, Inc., in care of Ms. Marilyn Polete, Secretary, with copies to Mrs. Jane Volk, Chairman, Landmarks Preservation Commission and Mr. John C. Randolph, Town Attorney, the following inclusions are of interest:

> "The original design (of the Chapel) took a form reminiscent of the colonial New England meetinghouse with two-tone white clapboard siding and a three-staged cupola/spire. The cupola/spire arrangement was flanked by a single story veranda with a hipped roof.

> Patrons to the church would pass through a large

aedicular entrance consisting of an arched opening
rising up through a broken triangular pediment. Inside
the visitor found a cruciform plan with an envelope of
light coming from the slender round-arched windows at
either side of the nave. Grand 'Palladian' or 'Venetian'
windows at the termination of the transept wings provided for an impressive source of light, flooding the body
of the church.

The large round-arched windows were double-hung
with a 12/12 glazing pattern. From early photographs,
it is evident that a dramatic landscape surrounded the
chapel. An arcuated drive wound its way through
flowers and palms up to the entrance of the church.
Photographs from the period indicate orientation to
the north.

An enlargement and renovation occurred around
1925. At that time, flat side sections were added to the
rear of the church. Also, windows were moved and
replaced, and side staircases were added.

In 1928, a tumultuous hurricane hit Palm Beach and
leveled the steeple. The storm also caused severe damage to the Royal Poinciana Hotel and other
structures in town. The spire was quickly gone. Although
attempts have been made over the years to replace the
tall cupola/spire arrangement, none of the plans have
come to fruition.

The Royal Poinciana Chapel was moved to a position in front of the Flagler estate, Whitehall, near the
east gates, around 1949. Photographs from the period
show the orientation toward the north, with a much
smaller semicircular drive leading up the foyer of the
Chapel.

The Chapel was moved for a second time in 1972 to
its present location at one of the highest points of land in
Palm Beach, on the Cocoanut Row frontage of the old

Brelsford property, some 400 feet away from its previous location. 'The move is being made in conjunction with the restoration of the original view from Whitehall - a landscaped view across Palm Beach, from the palatial Flagler estate to The Breakers Hotel on the ocean.' The Chapel was also turned ninety degrees and oriented to the east. The lot was considered quite safe due to the fact that the new resting place would be atop a coral reef. During this time, a complete renovation and restoration of the building was undertaken, under the direction of the architectural office of John Stetson.

Although a second steeple was not executed, it was intended. Proposals included the addition of a spire arrangement reminiscent of the works of Sir Christopher Wren, the renowned English architect responsible for the rebuilding of some 50 parish churches in London after the Great Fire of 1666. A request made to the Town Council to replace a spire in its new location was approved by the council but turned down by the board. The architects responded with a simple, yet adequate, ornamental tower block capped by a balustrade with pedestals and urns. The Chapel was also lowered to ground level at its new location, eliminating the steps that had to be negotiated by members of the congregation at the old location."

From the report one would think that the transition went smoothly. However, there were problems. Hank McCall's Whistle Tooting history touches briefly on some of what caused contention among the congregants and the community: "In 1966 we moved to buy the Maibach property, which was the old Brelsford house. John Stetson spearheaded that, and after many bitter arguments, he and Sam Lindsay got the congregation to go along with the purchase for $146,000. We were getting robbed! We bought it from a man named John Maibach. We were stuck with it. In 1967 the Flagler Museum purchased the lot we were on from the Florida East Coast Hotel and they gave us a five year lease for $1 a year. In 1966, John Stetson made a sketch from a theoretical plot plan. There (was) the Flagler Museum, ... the new Chapel with two or three buildings in the

Board of Trustees 1967. Front left to right John Stetson, Dr. Lindsay. Second Row left Tom Sperry, Delman 'Breezy' Wynn (with glasses), Arthur Heiser, Seward Patterson, Alvin Boettcher, Carl Eiser. Behind and right of Carl Eiser, Charles Koos, Algot Johnson. Third Row, Francis Dittrich, Herbert Adair, Unidentified, Robert Rooke, Vernon Raedisch, Hank McCall. Fourth Row, George Coleman, Arthur Gee, Unidentified, J.Y. Arnold, Sr., Unidentified and Dr. Stanley Inman

center... and a yacht club. Well, the Garden Club got it, the Civic Association got it and this inflamed them."

No one anticipated the outcry that pursued. At one of the more vocal meetings, against the opposition, Dr. Lindsay pled the cause thusly, according to Marilyn Polete, "Shoot if you must, this old grey head, but save the Chapel."

Hank's history interpretation and Dr. Lindsay's dramatic plea for continuance are confirmed in an article dated February 22, 1967 in the **Daily News**:

"Pros and Cons Fly on Chapel Zoning

Strong opposition broke out at a jam-packed meeting of the Town Zoning Commission Tuesday afternoon against rezoning a new site for The Royal Poinciana Chapel and against rezoning 117 Brazilian Ave. as an apartment house site.

The Carl Eisers, Dr. Lindsay and Dr. Inman with congregants 1967

The Palm Beach Civic Association and the Garden Club of Palm Beach figured largely in the opposition to the Chapel site rezoning plan. But the Chapel application for rezoning also had its adherents and speakers on both sides got loud applause from the standing-room-only crowd.

Speaking against the rezoning, Gavin Letts, member of the planning committee of the Civic Association inveighed against 'The commercial rape of this community.' 'Does the congregation intend to go down to the sea to do business with the Almighty or with the almighty dollar?'

Mrs. Dorothy DePeyster, president of the Garden

RICHARD LITTLE STUDIO

Board of Directors April 1972. Seated left to right, Algot Johnson, Carl Eiser, Alvin Boettcher
Standing from left, Arthur Heiser, Kenneth Richmond, Hank McCall, Arthur Gee, Herbert Chase

Club, also opposed any change in rezoning for a new Chapel site. She said the Garden Club 'is interested in preserving Palm Beach as a community of homes.'

A strenuous plea for more facilities for young people's recreation and religious teaching was made by J. Y. Arnold, Sr., an officer of the Chapel for 30 years. He said he'd rather see the Chapel remain in its present location but that its trustees had been told it would have to move in five years.

Arnold said there is no place, except for some small facilities, at the Church of Bethesda-by-the-Sea for the 1,000 or 1,500 Palm Beach children to go for wholesome recreation and Sunday School teaching here. 'We send our children across the lake to Sunday School because we can't look after them in Palm Beach.'

Vernon Raedisch, another Chapel trustee, said the Chapel wants only to remain in the same approximate location with more parking facilities and a better entrance for the Museum."

A bulletin was issued titled: ROYAL POINCIANA CHAPEL, Report of the Building Committee, Richard P. Scott, Alvin W. Boettcher, Carleton Smith, Report by Brig. Gen. Richard P. Scott, Chairman.

Its' contents explain the ultimate approval and planned renovation and removal of the Chapel after a period of diplomacy as explained by Hank McCall: "We were given two black eyes at that meeting (of the zoning board). There was no chance that we were ever going to move. But Sam Lindsay, with his charm,

Ushers 1986 from left: Arthur Gee, President Chapel Trustees, Carl Eiser, Algot Johnson, Arthur Heiser, Hank McCall, Alvin Boettcher, Head Usher

SAM R. QUINCEY

and 'Bay' Gee, with his patient, patient way, went to work and Marshall Criser, the Chapel attorney who was later president of Florida University, finally came up with a special exception and we moved."

The building committee's report outlines the potential move:

> "On June 8, 1971, the Town Council approved our Application for Special Exception in which we asked to move the existing Chapel on to adjacent property owned by us to the south... The approval was granted 'subject' to the providing of a 30 foot buffer along the south edge of the property, and subject to the requirement that there be no additional construction other than the moving of the existing Chapel and its appurtenances."

"On August 3, 1971, two members of our Building Committee, accompanied by our architect, met with... Building Official and the Fire Chief of the Town of Palm Beach. We were assured that the Town will cooperate in every way, in view of the historical value of the Chapel."

"It was determined that in order to comply with the Town noise ordinance restrictions and heavy construction, such as bulldozing and rock cutting... required to prepare the new site... must be accomplished prior to December 1, or be delayed until May 1, 1972. The un-interrupted construction period of May 1st onward will give us sufficient time to have the Chapel ready for its annual opening in late October for the 1972/73 season."

"As to preliminary plans, ... making such modifications and alterations as are necessary to meet the building codes. At the same time, it is necessary to perform long and neglected maintenance and repairs; and it is desirable to improve the exterior and interior appearance, as the budget permits."

"In effect, the Chapel is to be moved in its entirety (less front porches) and placed on a concrete foundation. The front of the Chapel is to be rebuilt to add a center foyer with required rest rooms off the main entrance. Open porches are to be restored in front. Elevation of the main entrance and side entrances will be two steps up. The proposed alterations, together with the addition of a properly proportioned steeple ... will serve to correct long existing architectural faults brought about by piecemeal additions and deletions in the past."

"...The new floor is to be covered with asphalt tile, except for the aisles which will be carpeted. Budget permitting, new pew seats are to be installed ... The choir and pulpit area is to be dressed up, improving the somewhat drab appearance ... We believe that this is the time to replace the square wooden columns with round steel columns covered with plaster, an action which has long been suggested as a means to improve visibility. ... It has been suggested by several that we remove the Little Chapel and administrative area altogether and build an extension to the rear of the Chapel."

MORT KAYE STUDIOS

James Y. Arnold, Sr. President of Board 1960 - 1964

"More urgent than adding to the existing Chapel is the need to repair and restore the present building ... we strongly suspect that we may have to replace the badly deteriorating roof ... Moreover, the amount of damage to wood siding and trim points more and more to the need for replacing it with wood or aluminum siding."

"At the Annual Meeting on April 1, 1971, the Trustees unanimously approved a motion 'that Mr. John Stetson be engaged as architect, providing a satisfactory contract could be negotiated.' And then, 'we are pleased to report that a satisfactory contract has been negotiated.'"

On January 11, 1972, James Arnold, Sr. sent a letter to "Members of Royal Poinciana Trustees" proffering a passionate plea to consider all the many benefits and practical aspects of building a "Replica Royal Poinciana Chapel" in an attempt to obviate all the problems associated with moving and maintaining the original old building. The letter suggests the plan is inadequate to serve a growing congregation, citing the intent to eliminate the wood siding and putting in toilets aside the front entry in a poorly conceived addition thereby losing the feeling of the old Chapel. James Arnold disputes the practicality of moving the old building when "a new masonry replica will reduce the cost of insurance, eliminate the need to destroy trees and tropical growth and to save the inconvenience of placing the old building too close to traffic on Cocoanut Row, leaving little room to landscape with the big trees that are needed to frame the Chapel and soften the noise, and to provide needed shade. The 'Loop' drive east of the Chapel is short and dangerous, and will return traffic too close to the entry ... future expansion is frozen at the east, south and north ... expansion can only go west which will most probably mean destruction of the historical White House."

A letter dated December 9, 1991 is addressed: Mr. Donald Carmichael, President, The Royal Poinciana Chapel. From C. H. McCall, it outlines a bit of the Chapel's history in regard to financing:

> "The Chapel borrowed $80,000 in 1967 from the First National Bank of Lake Worth to finance the $140,000 purchase of its present property. Even though they proposed to pay back $16,000 per year in five years, the mortgage was paid off in two years.
>
> The estimated costs of moving the Chapel were $250,000 to $300,000. As you can see from Dr. Lindsay's letter, work was contracted with only $120,000 of cash and pledges. Borrowing was planned but unnecessary because of a $10,000 gift from the Kenan Foundation and a $92,000 bequest from Mr. Seward Paterson. In this case, fortune smiled on the brave."

Another letter of interest is addressed "Dear Dr. Lindsay:" Hand-written on THE HENRY MORRISON FLAGLER MUSEUM stationery, it explains, "We missed you ... at the Life and Charter dinner. Please put the date in your book for the first Friday in February. Thank you so much for your most generous gift to the museum. I hope all plans for moving the Chapel are pretty well made and when settled I shall send you a contribution ... Jean Flagler Matthews, Whitehall Way, Palm Beach."

The transfer of the Chapel was performed by LaPlant Adair,

Outdoor service with Dr. Lindsay at lectern

sub-contractors. Nora Construction Company was the contractor and John Nora would ultimately devote many years to maintaining the old wooden Chapel.

When the preparation work was performed, the wooden shell of the old Chapel, cut in two sections, was hoisted onto wheels and rolled to the Maibach property. The Florida East Coast Railway paid the fee for removal. During the move, according to Hank, "we had services at the Whitehall, the Poinciana Playhouse and St. Edward's Parish House. The picture of Dr. Lindsay preaching on the lawn was one service during the interim period. The congregation slipped in numbers at that time. Dr. Lindsay was in his late eighties and he was not able to attract the crowds that we formerly had."

More controversy on the horizon. The **Palm Beach Daily News** on Sunday, June 17, 1973, contains a photograph of the exterior and interior of the Brelsford house. The headline read, "The Brelsford House - No Funds So It Faces Razing."

> "The historic Brelsford House, located next to the Royal Poinciana Chapel, will be torn down this summer ... The Chapel's trustees have decided they can't afford to keep the house ... built for Palm Beach's first postmaster, Edmund Munger Brelsford, in <u>1899</u> at a cost of $13,000, needs $10,000 in repair work to make it even 'liveable,' Mrs. Mary Polete, spokesman for the board said.

'We have no use for the house, neither as a Sunday School building nor as a minister's house ... It has bad sewage and plumbing problems and its quite a fire trap ...

The Historic Brelsford House

HISTORIC AMERICAN BUILDINGS SURVEY

the Chapel board, which owns the property, has faced multiple problems repairing vandalism to the structure.

Serious negotiations are under way to sell most of the inside woodwork and other salvageable items ... but none of the trees will be knocked down ... we intend to make the site into a garden, extending from the Chapel to the lake ... we have had several different groups who want to restore the house, but when they found out how much it would cost, they changed their minds.'

The Brelsford house, also called The Banyans, was part of the Historic American Buildings Survey of 1971.

Circuit Judge James R. Knott and other Palm Beachers who want to preserve local historical landmarks, are distressed over the prospect of losing the Greek Revival mansion.

'We tried to get the Flagler Museum to give permission

143

to move it on their property, but it's so large they don't think there's room for it there,' said Judge Knott.

The 13-bedroom home represents the height of general building construction before the modern Spanish style became popular. On the property is a Ceiba tree, imported from Nassau by Brelsford in 1890, the oldest and one of the two largest trees in Palm Beach.

In May 1880 E. M. and J. H. Brelsford came to the Lake Worth area, and bought up the Frank Dimick property, including the land on which both the Brelsford house and the Flagler Museum now stand.

George G. Matthews

The Brelsford brothers built a store on Brelsford's point (now Flagler's point) in 1884, marking the site of the beginning of Palm Beach. E. M. Brelsford became the postmaster of the post office January 15, 1887, naming it Palm City. On October 1, 1887, the name was changed to Palm Beach.

Henry Morrison Flagler came to Palm Beach in March of 1893. After a three-day stay, Mr. Flagler bought a strip of land out of the Brelsford's property, including the point and the store for $50,000. After Flagler built the Royal Poinciana Hotel in 1894 and nearby 'Whitehall' in 1901, the Brelsford house was built, sometime in 1902-1903." (Note the news article contradicts the building date).

From the time of the request by Jean Flagler Matthews that the Chapel be moved, through the actual move and the razing of the Brelsford House, there was much dissension but there was far more agreement and cooperation. However, it took five years of patience,

MORT KAYE STUDIOS

The big move. Note Little chapel and Organ Loft on rear.

perseverance and the skill of Arthur Gee and Dr. Lindsay among others. Some members of the Chapel felt that the duties of the Chapel
were to provide a Sunday School and a fellowship hall. They wanted
to erect new buildings, including a replica of the old structure, all for
a cost of $500,000. However, a conservative opinion won the vote and
after the congregation spent $250,000, the reconstructed Chapel was
dedicated on April 15, 1973.

During the actual moving and renovating, Marilyn Polete
remembers that she "performed the secretarial duties on the front
porch of the manse on Seaview Avenue and Dr. Lindsay performed
weddings, often free of charge, in the garden in back of the small

house at 437 Seaview. He performed the marriage of Mary Alice Firestone among other simple, but joyful weddings. Upon completion of the work I returned to the office area, two small rooms located at the rear of the sanctuary off of the Little Chapel."

A new location, a renovated Chapel and an aging Dr. Lindsay looked to the future ... and hopefully, as the fine old gent was wont to say: "The best days of the Chapel are ahead of us, not behind us."

Time marching on and the threads of lives continue to entwine and commit to the furtherance of God's work through the ministers, the congregants and even the descendants of Henry Flagler. Jean Flagler Matthews died in 1979. Her son, George G. Matthews, great grandson of Henry Flagler, recalls that Henry Flagler died when his mother was an infant and, therefore, had little recollection of her grandfather. Raised as a member of Bethesda-by-the Sea, where he sang in the choir, George would ultimately join the Chapel and become actively involved as a member of the Board of Spiritual Managers as well as a member of the Board of Directors, in addition to his continuing commitment to Whitehall as Chairman of the Board of Trustees for the museum - the magnificent mansion that Henry Flagler built in 1902 for Mary Lily. George Matthews fully appreciates the unique ancestral lineage, a divine prophecy that binds him unequivocally to the Little White Church by the Trail.

Dr. John U. Miller

$\mathcal{D}$R. MILLER —
A BRIDGE BETWEEN

Bill Tell came to Palm Beach after retiring in 1971 from his executive position with Marathon Oil Company. Bill and wife Virginia met after a Dartmouth-Northwestern football game in 1928. They raised two sons and investigated both Arizona and California before retiring to Palm Beach - inspired by a Christmas holiday visit to the island at the invitation of Bill's former boss at Marathon, Arthur "Bay" Gee.

Bill, born in Grand Rapids, Michigan in 1907, was the only child of a father who was auditor for Standard Oil Company. The Flagler alliance continued to weave its threads through the Chapel history in prophetic turns. There were many moves for the Tells due to business and Bill attended eighteen different grammar schools. He started high school in Peoria but after three months the family settled in Chicago, where Bill completed high school and then enrolled at Northwestern University to study law. His law degree was awarded in 1931 and he practiced in the "windy city" for ten years before going with Marathon Oil in Findlay, Ohio as legal counsel. He traveled the world for Marathon and was ready to settle in one place upon retiring.

Associated with the First Methodist Church of Findlay, the Tells attended services at the Methodist Church in West Palm before succumbing to the ministrations of Dr. Lindsay. It was "Bay" Gee, loyal Board Member of the Chapel, who inspired Bill to serve on the board as well.

However, he was not yet President of the board in November 1971 when the Sunday bulletin spoke so eloquently to the hearts of the many congregants. The music that Sunday began with César Franck's Prelude Fugue and Variations played by organist Murray Fastier. The hymn, "Our God, Our Help in Ages Past" was followed by the Scripture lesson, then an anthem, "God Is a Spirit," then the Call to Prayer and Sweet Hour of Prayer. Dr. Lindsay's sermon, "Three Necessary Sailors" was next and then the hymn, "Guide Me, O Thou Great Jehovah." The bulletin also contained a page of inspirational pieces. They are classic Sam Lindsay:

> "The historical Chapel on the Trail is one of God's service stations on the highway of life. Here we get a renewal of our spiritual resources, courage to face reality, and confidence in the ultimate victory of righteousness. Here we gain a new appreciation of Jesus Christ and a clearer understanding of the eternal truth He taught.
>
> GOOD FRIENDS
>
> Let us pray that strength and courage abundant be given to all who work for a world of reason and understanding; that the good that lies in every man's heart may day by day be magnified; that men will come to see more clearly not that which divides them, but that which unites them; that each hour may bring us closer

to a final victory, not of nation over nation but of many over his own evils and weaknesses; that the blessings of peace be ours - the peace to build and grow, to live in harmony and sympathy with others, and to plan for the future with confidence."

And a poem followed: "BROTHERHOOD

There is a destiny that makes us brothers;
None goes his way alone:
All that we send into the lives of others
Comes back into our own.
I care not what his temples or his creeds,
One thing holds firm and fast -
That into his fateful heap of days and deeds
The soul of man is cast.

— Edwin Markham"

The attendance was slipping when Dr. John U. Miller came from Louisville to assist the aging preacher as he entered his last decade. Bill Tell recalls a time when Dr. Lindsay was speaking to a thousand or fifteen hundred each Sunday in season. It was then when the gentle Scot with the wonderful sense of humor left Florida for three or four months to preach at Lake Placid and visit his dear friends in Brookline, loyal, intrepid fans.

Bill Tell describes the Chapel as "merely a preaching station for Sam Lindsay - a place for him to hold fort. Dr. Lindsay loved the sound of his own voice and his sermons were wonderful but he got so he didn't know when to quit. The service became strictly a lengthy conversation, rambling but entertaining and inspirational."

It was Bill Tell who convinced Dr. Lindsay that Palm Beach needed the fourth church as a year-round church. Dr. Lindsay wasn't particularly in favor of the suggestion but, after many discussions with Bill, agreed that he would conduct services one summer on a trial basis. If the average attendance was at least a hundred, he would consider remaining in Palm Beach for the entire year.

According to Bill, "When the attendance did average a hundred worshippers it became a year-round church. This is particularly significant in that the Chapel, the first church on the island, is the foundation for all the churches in Palm Beach. What is also unique about the Chapel is that *the people run it* rather than the minister."

In the early eighties the members of the Chapel became embroiled in conflict that sorely wrenched the very foundation of the small white edifice, nearly destroying every semblance of that which Dr. Lindsay so eloquently preached of Brotherhood, Forgiveness and Tolerance. And Dr. Miller became centered in the controversy at a time when Dr. Lindsay was fading from the scene.

"When Dr. Miller arrived," according to then Board President Hank McCall, "Dr. Lindsay became Minister Emeritus, but was reluctant to let go of the power and influence that he had enjoyed for thirty years." Barbara Pearson Johnson recalls those tumultuous times explaining that it was like a vacuum, "Dr. Lindsay couldn't (perform his duties) and Dr. Miller wouldn't. Dr. Miller suffered from intimidation and Dr. Lindsay would not yield authority to make decisions. It was a most difficult circumstance for Dr. Miller."

With background music becoming discordant, Marilyn Polete remembers, "Dr. Miller was a fine man who had the most wonderful command of the English language — an outstanding orator with a wonderful voice. Because Dr. Lindsay was still in demand, he alternated speaking every other Sunday with Dr. Miller. There was a definite division in the congregation with each man's fans attending their favorite minister's service." Enter into this divided congregation, Organist and new Minister of Music, Thomas R. Thomas. Marilyn, having witnessed many transitions over the years, reports that with each new organist there seemed to be an attempt to revise or embellish the old Chapel organ. The organ certainly held a vital role in the Chapel history as reported by devout member and Chapel historian, Robert G. Murray, in an article that fully outlines the history of the organ. An accompanying letter from Thomas sets the scene.

The informative letter to Jack Jones, dated January

30, 1997, is headed: THOMAS - PIERCE LIMITED

Organ Architects, Consultants and Restorers, Member American Institute of Organ Builders, Representing Austin Organs, Inc.

"Jack,

Here is an accurate article written by Bob Murray at a time the Austin was installed in the Chapel. We have discovered since that the Odell organ from Whitehall was combined with an existing one manual organ that preceded the Möeller. This organ was opus 263 built by C. E. Morey of Utica, New York around 1909. It is interesting that Bethesda also had a Morey opus 273 built in 1910 in their old building.

1. The first instrument used in the Chapel was a reed organ by Mason & Hamlin
2. C. E. Morey (one manual) installed c. 1909 (probably purchased by Flagler). (A hand-written note: this was given to Graham Eckes School and has since disappeared.)
3. M. P. Möeller installed 1963
4. Austin Organ opus 2685 (utilizing Möeller parts and pipes) 1984 (signed) Thom Thomas"

The brief history by Murray was written for the American Organist and titled: THE ROYAL POINCIANA CHAPEL ORGANS, PALM BEACH. Excerpts include unique descriptive qualities to enhance the understanding of the ultimate music accompaniment at the Chapel.

"The first organ in the Chapel was a Mason & Hamlin Vocalion with an elaborate facade. A Professor Kahn of Jacksonville dedicated the new organ in December 1895 during the Chapel's first wedding service. The organ was played on Sunday mornings by Flagler's organist-in-residence Russell T. Joy, who was responsible for the 1901 Odell tubular-pneumatic organ in the music room of Whitehall. The first organ must have been particularly without strength, as both Mr. Joy and subsequent organists complained about its inadequacies.

Sometime after Flagler's death in 1913, his mansion was sold. The Odell organ was removed and given to the Chapel. This organ, unaltered excepting the electrification of the tubular-pneumatic action, was attached to a three-manual Reisner console. The installation in the Chapel was unfortunate; rather than adapt the building to accept the organ, a box-like structure was built behind the chancel, attached to the exterior of the building.

During 1961, Rev. Samuel M. Lindsay, decided to replace the Odell using a bequest from the Myron and Annabelle Taylor Foundation. The Odell was returned to Whitehall and replaced in the music room by Jean Flagler Matthews. Bids for a new organ were sought from Austin, Möeller, Aeolian-Skinner and Wicks companies. Möeller was chosen; they built Opus 9720, consisting of 32 ranks and four divisions, placed in a similar manner as the Odell had been, in an even larger exterior extension to the rear of the Chapel. The installation included a small antiphonal division of four ranks in the steeple tower. The contract was signed January 25, 1962, for the sum of $50,917, with Carleton Bullis serving as the Chapel's consultant.

Almost immediately it was realized that the same problem which had plagued the earlier instruments, buried in attached chambers, incapable of tonal grandeur - also afflicted this installation.

During the 1972 move and renovation of the Chapel, another opportunity was overlooked to bring the organ into the building and reinstall it properly. Instead, in an effort to have the organ serve both the main sanctuary and a small chapel used for weddings, it was removed further from the interior and suffered a corresponding decrease in tonal quality and volume.

Thomas R. Thomas was appointed Director of music at the Chapel in 1978 and at his urging, Virgil Fox was invited to be artist-in-residence. The two shared the same console and put their heads together to design an organ capable of playing all periods of literature.

At a 1981 meeting, the Chapel addressed the problems of the deterioration of the console: operated by wind, with many leather parts, its problems were becoming apparent during services. Several leathers damaged by mice were shown and a motion was made to supply the organist with a mousetrap. A. Guy Freas spoke with Thomas concerning the replacement of the console and along with wife Louise, Mr. Freas underwrote the purchase for a new Austin four-manual console. The generosity of the Freas Foundation was the impetus to set the organ project in motion."

There was strong opposition to the new organ, Dr. Lindsay for one felt the existing organ to be satisfactory. However, the Murray organ history goes on to outline just what did transpire in spite of growing tumult within the Chapel.

"The first of the planned addition of 58 voices, a Festival Trumpet, was installed temporarily in January 1983; it is now positioned horizontally on the rear gallery case as a Trompette en Chamade. Plans for the completed organ were unveiled, and Robert L. Rooke offered to give half the funds necessary, providing that the congregation and friends would raise the other half, and that the organ be installed during the Chapel's centennial year of 1984.

By early August 1983, the new organ was shipped in a large moving van, which arrived in Palm Beach August 9. The normally sedate Chapel became a beehive of activity, with musicians, tuners and voicers, carpenters, electricians, cabinetmakers, hoisters and riggers, and a host of others trooping in and out of the historic church. The dedicatory concert was given by Mr. Thomas on March 4, 1984."

However smooth the installation may appear from written words, it held dissonance beyond anyone's imaginings as chords of discontent engulfed the Chapel.

The turbulent episode that so sadly split the church is explained to some degree by the Minutes of the meetings during the early eighties. The troubling demons in the hearts and minds of man can only be imagined and forgiven over time.

A report to the Trustees of the Chapel, dated March 22, 1982, from the Chairman of the Music Committee, Robert G. Murray, outlines his devotion to the Chapel and to its history:

"OUR MUSIC HISTORY IS RICH! We are the oldest religious organization in old Dade County, and ... even Mary Lily Flagler sang at our services. In recent years, we were fortunate enough to have Virgil Fox as Artist-in-Residence, former organist of the Riverside Church in New York City and considered the World's Most Famous Organist. I recall that during his concert at the Chapel, he stood and spoke to the audience with his hand over his mouth (to muffle the sound of his voice) and explained to us what the problem with our installation is ... SOMEDAY there will be a complete orchestra again, within the confines of the organ's chambers and we will have not only the finest accompaniment to our worship, but an attraction for the entire area that will reflect our appreciation of the Glory of God through music. SOMEDAY, very soon, the first part of this project will become a reality. The only remaining four manual draw-knob console in Palm Beach County will be installed through the gift of Mr. and Mrs. A. Guy Freas. Also, at that time, preparations have been made for the restoration of the Festival Trumpet, this important stop used for weddings, funerals and other celebrations. It would be my pleasure to provide the funds necessary for the installation of this portion of the project in memory of my grandmother, Catherine Frances Murray. A complete specification for the proposed additions to the organ has been designed by Mr. Thomas, using Dr. Fox's notes and with the capable assistance of Commodore Pierce. It has been submitted to Austin Organs of Hartford for a formal proposal."

A letter from Robert L. Rooke dated November 23, 1982 confirmed his "commitment made at lunch given by Mrs. Louise Freas, to give $175,000 (half the contract price) to purchase and install a new organ. This pledge provisional upon the members of the congregation, friends of the Chapel and members of the Board of Trustees providing the other $175,000 in time to install the organ and have it operating for the one hundredth anniversary of the Chapel in 1984."

Hank McCall, President of the Board, wrote a letter to Robert L. Rooke thanking him for the generous offer, "... received with joyous appreciation. This challenge should put a lot of spark in the members of our Chapel." However, Hank amended the letter with "your pledge is provisional upon the members of the congregation, friends of the Chapel and the Board first raising their $175,000 in assets and bonafide pledges... If the Chapel decides to scale down the size of the new organ contract, your pledge will decrease proportionally."

Mr. and Mrs. Robert Rooke

MORT KAYE STUDIOS

Hank McCall confesses that he was unaccustomed to working with committees having been in the life insurance business since 1964 as an individual salesman with no experience of chairing meetings. He had succeeded Bill Tell as President.

The Board of Directors met on January 17, 1983 and among other issues discussed was Mr. Rooke's letter and the visit with Mr. Rooke by President McCall and Hugh Pierce to discuss the pledge for the new organ. "Mr. Rooke imposed a time limitation ... 'I may not be around much longer and I'd like to hear it!'" He would ultimately hear the organ for four or five years but only after the wrenching brouhaha was put to rest.

The meeting, like the one in February, was attended by guests Hugh M. Pierce, Chairman of the Music Committee and Thomas R. Thomas, Organist. A presentation of the Music Committee gave a summary of the proposal with architectural renderings by Austin Organ Company and John Stetson. "William Tell suggested that the pulpit be centered in the chancel, not on the side, as rendering indicated." When several members felt that the amount of $175,000 could be manageable, Hank McCall proposed that a letter of intent to Austin with a check be submitted. William Tell proposed a motion to that affect, seconded by R. H. Kirkpatrick."

At the meeting in February Hugh Pierce reported an anonymous gift of $5,000 toward the organ fund. Hugh Pierce recommended signing the contract with Austin Organ Co. H. Richard Williams commented concerning Mr. Pierce's presentation at Sunday Service, stating he was not speaking for the Board of Directors. William Tell stated that the message was pressuring members for pledges and was disturbing: "The Organ fund would reduce Easter offering this year." Mr. Tell also remarked that "the organ's value is equal to the Chapel edifice ... Some members are opposed to the expenditure." H. Richard Williams moved to proceed with signing of contract. Roy C. Moersch recommended that the Chapel not go into debt. Also discussed was a fee to Thomas Thomas, customary for supervising the installation of the console.

The passions were building and the chasm deepening.

To ameliorate the opposition, a report by Robert G. Murray, Chairman of Building and Grounds Committee, given March 1983, praises the Trustees regarding the current status of "our Historic Meetinghouse and Property during this year of preparation for our hundredth anniversary. "As steward of this property, I'd like to voice my deep appreciation to all of you (he lists Dr. Sam Lindsay and Hank McCall) who have kept this house of God here in this place." The report continues, "I'm certain that all will be relieved that the huge piles of debris from the restoration of the waterfront project which is under way and the general trimming has now disappeared ... Many work crews have been on the property ... The building needs cleaning and repainting. The lawn will require a good fertilizing ... The Virgil Fox memorial circle has already been funded by a gift ... Most importantly, the building interior and exterior has been added to by the gifts of a lighted celtic cross at the entrance and the new organ to be installed this summer."

A report issued by the Music Committee gave witness to a suggestion by a board member, "to establish a 'tradition' that the Benediction and Seven-fold Amen written by Peter Lutkin be incorporated as a permanent element of the worship service." The member further stated that he had been having a "running fight" over this matter and, while the Peter Lutkin piece is occasionally sung, he wished to insure that it be sung at the close of the service every Sunday and that further, the member intends to pursue this matter to a conclusion satisfactory to him and if the Music Committee is not the proper forum then he intends to bring the matter to the Board of Directors."

A report of the Music Committee at the Annual Meeting of the Board for March 22, 1983 stressed: "By far, the most important events of the past year have been the installation of the new organ console and your overwhelming support of the organ expansion program." Respectfully submitted, Hugh M. Pierce, Music Committee.

At the April 26th meeting of the Board "William Tell presented his ideas for Choral Meditation, 'The Lord Bless You' to be included as a permanent part of the Sunday Worship." "Robert G.

Murray commented on alterations to Chapel - lowering choir platform. William Tell does not feel this is a time to consider the plan."

At the same meeting President McCall presented the subject of Sea Gull Cottage - "soon to be either moved or demolished. Mr. Earl E. T. Smith, President of the PRESERVATION FOUNDATION OF PALM BEACH, INC. approached Dr. Miller with certain proposals for moving Sea Gull Cottage to Chapel grounds."

"President McCall suggested that Mrs. Edwin Glass, a building contractor, formerly of Washington, D. C., serve on that committee. Mrs. Glass is a member of the Chapel."

The financial outlay for the organ and demands made by members for and against, only further divided the split congregation. When tempers clashed in meetings it seemed the Chapel would not survive. However, in an attempt to hold together, and with Dr. Miller's blessing and support, Alicia Engle instigated the hospitality after service for congregants to meet and greet one another on the lawn behind the Chapel or in the Little Chapel behind the sanctuary. In the opinion of one member, the intended application was misused as an opportunity to air differences and further incite opposing camps. Alicia Engle and other members also gave some "splendid parties in their homes." Hank McCall remembers the affairs where wonderful food and drink was enjoyed and stories told and in his opinion, "the parties helped hold the Chapel together during the tumult."

Another creative fund-raiser, instigated by Hank, was inspired by Rome Hartman and designed to get people together. Dubbed the Bishop's Chicken Fund Raiser, having a definite Catholic flavor, the feast was held at the Beach Club where Bill Tell picked up the tab while Hank delivered an entertaining talk. Hank doesn't recall how much money was raised but he says the Chapel has always been "gloriously solvent," and through the period of extreme unrest, "the generosity of the wealthy attendees continued to support the Chapel."

One particularly generous gift came later and under rather extraordinary circumstances, but gives witness to the generosity.

Hank relates, "Mr. O. Ray Moore, of Atlanta, told me that he wanted to make a substantial gift of his company's stock to the Chapel, earmarked for the 'Samuel Lindsay Memorial Fund.' Mr. Moore further directed, "We will make it a Monday, Tuesday, Wednesday deal." Hank questioned, "And how does that work?"

"On Monday I will give the Chapel shares of my stock. On Tuesday, I will sell my company to a large insurance company. On Wednesday, the insurance company will buy the stock from the Chapel. It must be understood that the Chapel will sell the stock." Hank was very pleased to acknowledge that, "All went smoothly and on Wednesday, $150,000 was put into the Memorial Fund."

The Board meeting, Tuesday, May 31, 1983 presided over by President Hank McCall concerned the Sea Gull Cottage. "The meeting was called to discuss the proposed donation of Sea Gull Cottage by Preservation Foundation of Palm Beach to Royal Poinciana Chapel in exchange for the Chapel providing an appropriate site for the building. Ambassador Earl E. T. Smith, Dr. John U. Miller, Robert G. Murray and Mrs. Edwin Glass had been appointed at the April meeting to study the subject. William Tell commented on the need for additional space for the Chapel for purposes of a social hall and Sunday School. He believed that to place Sea Gull on property of the Chapel would be a mistake, but did suggest use of the circle just west and north of the Chapel.

Robert Murray revealed many historical facts at the meeting and commented that the circle was originally a part of the Flagler Museum property purchased some years before from the Museum.

Ambassador Smith commented that the most difficult part of the Preservation Foundation's deal was to convince the Board of Directors.

Subject of religious speakers during the Centennial Year 1984 was discussed. Richard Williams reported that Rev. Jerry Falwell will speak on Tuesday, January 17. R. H. Kirkpatrick reported that Rev. Norman Vincent Peale regretted, by letter, that he was unable to speak at the Chapel. Other well known religious leaders will be contacted to fill speaking engagements during year 1984 - 100 year celebration."

A letter from Earl E. T. Smith, Chairman, Preservation Foundation to Board of Directors, Royal Poinciana Chapel, articulates the proposal for the return of Flagler's first home on the island to a place very close to where it was originally built for Mr. McCormick, and very close to where the original Chapel was built in 1897/1898.

"Gentlemen: The Preservation Foundation proposes to donate the Sea Gull Cottage to the Royal Poinciana Chapel in exchange for the Chapel providing an appropriate site for the building. The Preservation Foundation would also request space for its office and monthly board meetings. This would mean a small room for a secretary and a larger room for the director. We should have a legal agreement from the Chapel to preserve and protect in perpetuity the restored appearance of the building, and right of first refusal to reacquire the building if the Chapel should ever decide to dispose of the property. Except for the space needed ... the rest of the cottage would be available to the Chapel to use as it wishes, subject to approval of the Town Council.

In return for providing the site, the Preservation Foundation will be responsible for all costs incurred in moving the cottage, site preparation and any necessary variances. The Preservation Foundation will also pay for the cost of exterior renovation including research, architectural and engineering fees and new construction, including up-to-date mechanical systems and utility hookups.

The Preservation Foundation has received a gift of $50,000 in honor of Philip N. Fortin, and we would ask that a plaque in his memory be located on or near the building.

The Sea Gull Cottage will not be vacant to move until April of 1984. We would plan to move it as soon after April 1 as possible. We hope that the cottage will be ready for occupancy within twelve months of the move and relocation.

The Preservation Foundation Looks forward to working with the Royal Poinciana Chapel on this historically significant project."

In spite of the good news regarding the return of Sea Gull, the infighting continued, culminating in serious allegations proffered by both sides. Finally, in an attempt to save the Chapel, Dr. Miller and the Board asked that certain members resign.

A letter from Clarence Henry McCall to the Board dated November 29, 1983 states: "Thank you for your time and service during these past hectic days.

Please enter in the records of meetings that I am opposed to and disagree with all resolutions and decisions of today's meeting.

It is my prayer that you have made the correct decisions. In my opinion, the actions today were too practical, rigid, and harsh. I strongly feel that courses based on love, forgiveness, and flexibility should have been tried first.

It is my intention to faithfully carry out the decision of the Board to the best of my ability.

Yours very truly, C. H. McCall"

In another letter from President McCall to the Board, dated December 5, 1983: "This is my protest against your decisions ... Since the Board has refused to allow (the accused) to speak in defense or advance specific reasons for their dismissal, a gross injustice has been done.

Please accept my resignation as President of the Trustees and from the board of Directors.

Yours very truly, C. H. McCall"

On December 5, 1983, a letter addressed to C. H. McCall, from R. H. Kirkpatrick, explains his intent:

"Please accept the resignation of the undersigned as Vice President, Treasurer and member of the Board of Directors ... I am not a candidate for return to any of those offices.

Should the incoming president of the Chapel prefer to appoint a person of his own choosing as Chairman of the Pulpit Search Committee, I shall willingly yield that assignment ..."

A letter from Dr. Miller to Mr. C. H. McCall is succinct:

"This is to advise you and the Board of Directors that I must, for reasons of health, officially retire from the active pastorate of the Chapel at the conclusion of 1984.

This will enable me to fulfill my commitments to the Chapel for the centennial celebration and make possible a proper period of time for your Search Committee to find a successor.

Moreover, I would like the written permission of the Board to publicly make the announcement of my retirement at the Annual Meeting of the congregation to be held at the Beach Club on March 2, 1984.

Your Pastor, Dr. John U. Miller"

In the midst of the tempest, Dr. Lindsay, still not in favor of replacing the organ, seemed quite unaware of the turmoil whirling round the Chapel. He was approaching his hundredth birthday at the same time that the 'Union Congregational Church at Palm Beach', precursor to the interdenominational Chapel, approached its 100th anniversary.

Lois Krueger remembers that Dr. Lindsay was in a wheelchair toward the end of his tenure. "The old gent could be difficult and while he was determined to preach, I must admit that age was taking a toll. It was sad for me to witness the decline of Dr. Lindsay, particularly when I knew so well how brilliant he had been in his prime." Lois recalls that "Marilyn, who he referred to as 'Virgin Mary', was like a daughter to him — caring for him and driving him wherever he wanted to go ... their relationship was very special. Dr. Lindsay lost his wife in December (of 1983) and we all tried to let him know how much we cared ... one day I went into the Chapel office ... Dr. Lindsay was there but could not hear very well nor was his vision good. I leaned over and whispered something to him and he acknowledged me as he always did, 'Oh, this is my joyful friend!'"

Unfortunately, it was a time when there was too much that was not joyful within the Chapel. Bob Kirkpatrick wrote a memo during this period: " ... In all candor I don't like much of the proposed program. I have said repeatedly that I do not want to be president and that I would refuse the assignment. I relent on that only because of what I perceive to be acutely serious circumstances for which there is no quick or easy solution ... I want my tenure as president to be as short as possible."

There were decisions to be made concerning a biography being prepared by Northwood Press in honor of Dr. Lindsay. There were delays and concern that it would not be completed in time to be available for the centennial celebration.

A letter of December 12, 1983 to the Board from R. H. Kirkpatrick confirms that the unrest was far from over: "Please accept the resignation of the undersigned as Vice President, Treasurer, Member of the Board of Directors, Chairman of the 100th Anniversary Committee and Chairman of the Pulpit Search Committee, effective this date.

I am not a candidate for return to any of these offices or committee assignments.

I submit this resignation without rancor but with unshakable conviction ... I must respectfully decline to preside over a policy I believe to be without justification or merit and harmful to the Chapel's future."

Minutes for the December 12, 1983 meeting contain motions that were approved but did not clear the air of mistrust.

"C. H. McCall's letter of resignation ... Amended to read that Mr. McCall is resigning from the Board of Directors ... motion moved by Mr. Tell and seconded by Mr. Johnson. Motion to reelect Mr. Kirkpatrick as President ... Mr. Kirkpatrick stated that he did not seek, nor want this position, however, if elected he will do the best he can with no commitment made to length of time. When Mr. Tell has completed his reorganization, hopefully a new president will be found."

Amidst the unrest, at the presentation of Emeritus Citation by

Bob Kirkpatrick to Dr. Lindsay in January of 1984, James R. Knott wrote a piece for the bulletin in Dr. Lindsay's honor:

Venerable Dr. Lindsay

DAVIDOFF STUDIOS

"THE RIGHT MAN IN THE RIGHT PLACE AT THE RIGHT TIME

The life of Samuel Macauley Lindsay is the story of a man of modesty and genius who, asking nothing but giving everything of himself to mankind, became one of the celebrated preachers and spiritual leaders of our time.

Through the years he formed warm relationships with other notable churchmen ... We love and treasure Dr. Lindsay. We honor him and try to obey his precepts, although we don't always succeed. We enjoy his company. We relish his moral strength and rely on it for spiritual support. We feel and learn from - his warm, engaging humanity.

Dr. Lindsay's humanity, born of superior discernment, insight and spirituality, engulfs those around him; it flows over them and inundates them. Practicing his favorite doctrines of forgiveness and Christian tolerance, he doesn't just love his fellow man, as a matter of principle; he likes us as well. With a total absence of negative attitudes towards others, he intuitively understands them and, understanding them, appreciates and enjoys them ... Much of our response lies in the joy and satisfaction derived from contact with a rare personality combining wisdom and original force coupled with a certain gentle charm. If we are fortunate, we may be inspired to emulate the qualities exemplified in this man.

The vigor and potency of Dr. Lindsay's character and personality has had a heroic impact, a lasting and enduring imprint for good upon our community. He has given new life to this Chapel and remade it into a significant community institution during a difficult period of important social changes.

His personal life provides us with an example to follow, not least in his selfless devotion to charitable causes. His whole being is oriented toward service to others. He is a man of many and varied talents ...

The rich scholarly achievements so clearly evident in Dr. Lindsay's sermons are reminiscent of certain other great preachers of America, including the late Dr. George Morgan Ward ...

Dr. Lindsay long ago dedicated himself to the proposition enunciated by Sir William Osler, the famous physician, that nothing in life is more wonderful than faith — 'the one great moving force which we can neither weigh in the balance nor test in the crucible.'

Dr. Lindsay's achievements have raised a monument which will always endure, exemplifying the adage that we are here to add what we can to life, not to get what we can from life. Paraphrasing Longfellow, he will leave his footprints on the sands of time.

Certain lines of John Greenleaf Whittier seem appropriate in our thoughts of Dr. Lindsay:

'O brother man, fold to thy heart thy brother;
where pity dwells, the peace of God is there;
To worship rightly is to love each other,
Each smile a hymn, each kindly deed a prayer.'"

Sadly, in spite of the glowing appraisal of Dr. Lindsay, giving testimony to his creed, the line of dissent within the Chapel was deepening when slanderous allegations were bandied about and reputations were at stake. Libel suits were threatened. In February the meetings spoke of rancor and threats and members shunning other members. It was all too much for Dr. Miller to abide. President Kirkpatrick attempted to bring peace and sanity back to the Chapel with a report praising Hank McCall for contributions through the last year:

> "These contributions were many. Selecting one of these as number one is difficult, but ranking very high is the creation of the Hospitality Committee. Operating under the enthusiastic and able direction of Alicia Engel, it is the group of Chapel members who serve Sunday morning refreshments to Chapel visitors.
>
> ... The Chapel's new organ project was approved and carried out under Hank's general direction, assisted greatly by the Chapel's Music Committee then under the Chairmanship of Hugh Pierce. This superior new instrument will strengthen and enlarge the Chapel's sphere of Christian influence for many years to come.
>
> It was at Hank's direction that a Centennial Observance Committee was established and still is in operation.
>
> Appearing intermittently throughout the year on the back of the Chapel's Sunday bulletins is a Chapel History series, authored by Bob Murray at the sugges-tion of Dr. Miller.
>
> Also set in motion during McCall's last year as President were the negotiations between the Chapel and the Preservation Foundation. The talks look to the possible relocating on Chapel property of the Sea Gull Cottage, the first Palm Beach Island home of Henry M. Flagler.
>
> These are the high points and the positive aspects of

the past year. Unfortunately, it is necessary to note that the Chapel also has been subjected to some unsettling influences and disturbing vexations. These have contributed to the departure after Easter Sunday of our Pastor, Dr. Miller. No successor is yet on the horizon but a further report in this area will be forthcoming from Dr. Robert Gronlund."

On March 5, 1984 the Board met and discussed Sea Gull Cottage regarding contract revision and details. William Tell read provisions as prime negotiator in setting up the form for the Board of Directors to be presented to Board of Trustees. The cottage is described in the Minutes: "A beautiful gift to the Chapel considering the cost; moratorium on building in Town of Palm Beach would not permit us to build; Town has approved location of cottage. If Chapel had to build there is no assurance of funds - it is this building or nothing, and we definitely need space."

"President Kirkpatrick discussed meeting with Dr. Gezork, who will be available through May. He *will not* be available in June. He will preach only — no responsibilities.

President Kirkpatrick stated that Rev. David W. Beebe might be available to continue Bible Class."

The Pastor's Annual Report from Dr. John U. Miller to the Board for 1983 is succinct particularly in light of all that occurred during his six-year pastorate at the Chapel.

"This represents a full six year record of pastoral responsibilities and relates to the growing strength of the Chapel and its many services to any and all persons of varied religious background. Let the record state that the church concept shows steady growth and the membership ... has passed the 400 mark. On the positive side this points toward a meaningful centennial year in 1984."

"However, there is a negative aspect to this Annual Report in that the pastor gave written notice of his intention to retire at the end of 1984. Regretfully, the birth-pains attendant upon the growing church concept for the Chapel has disclosed a current power struggle affecting the Board's and the Pastor's functions. Because of this the retirement date has been accelerated to Easter, April 22, 1984. May the resolution of differences see the Chapel and its Board blessed in the future under its new directed leadership.

With firm prayers, I am, Your Pastor, John U. Miller"

A report from President Kirkpatrick begins: "Changing times ... troubled times. Much travail already ... probably more ahead ... convinced that Chapel will prevail, will survive and regain the serenity and goodwill so long it's characteristic. Not every person here believes that; a few are forecasting certain doom. Some threaten to desert, a few already have. Some cite Scripture to justify their decisions. With the kindliest of feelings for those who would walk out, I can cite Scriptural admonitions to fight the good fight in the face of adversity, not to pass by on the other side of the road.

...I did not seek, did not want this assignment. Agreed to take it and intend to do the best I can towards fulfilling what I perceive to be its responsibilities, trying always to remember to base attitudes and efforts on facts and not allegations and innuendoes. Will not seek to dictate policy, will endeavor only to help formulate it and execute the collective decisions.

... Goals will be difficult, attainment, will take time; demand commitment and dedication by everyone.

First absolutely No. 1 goal is the acquiring of an experienced, superior and compassionate preacher, one who will help us fill the Chapel pews as they were filled to overflowing in an earlier era."

As the committee continued its search for Dr. Miller's replacement, and the battle raged within the Chapel walls, there were other preachers and the ever-present message of peace and love and forgiveness emanated from the pulpit. There was also a very special tribute to Dr. Lindsay.

The bulletin for Sunday, January 1, 1984 holds a photograph of a portrait of Dr. Lindsay and inside a biography. The heading follows: "Celebration of Worship, ONE CENTURY - JUST A BEGINNING," then the written hope "Whosoever thou art that entereth this church, remember it is the house of God. Be reverent; be attentive; be thoughtful; and leave it not without prayer to God, for thyself, for those who minister, and those who worship here."

Under the heading

"ANNOUNCEMENTS AND ACTIVITIES

Tuesday - 10:30 - Prayer-Healing Service and Holy Communion

Wednesday - 10:30 - Bible Lectures in Little Chapel - Madge Yoakley , Instructor

Thursday - 10:30 - Bible Lectures - Marcella Miller

WELCOME DR. GEZORK

In the celebration of the beginning of the 100th anniversary of the Chapel a Resolution and document conferring Emeritus status is being presented to Dr. Lindsay. Dr. Herbert Gezork, former President of Andover-Newton Theological Seminary is preaching the sermon this morning.

MEMORIAL FLOWERS

The poinsettias are given in loving memory of ALVIN W. BOETTCHER by his wife, Muriel.

The Flowers on the pedestals are given to the glory of God and in loving memory of EDMUND H. TAYLOR by Harold Masten."

The last page of the bulletin holds a prayer:

"O Lord God, if this is a strange and singular world to us, full of mysteries, sorrows, and enigmas we cannot explain, if we are tantalized by happenings whose meanings are hidden and by anomalies in nature, if there are veils we cannot tear aside and dreams we cannot interpret enable us humbly to recognize that Thy ways are higher than our ways and Thy thoughts than our thoughts. Yet we would not rest satisfied. Teach us the way of daily inquiry. Enable us always to keep on 'the line of discovery:' May knowledge grow from more to more. Thou dost make secrets of things to show them to us more plainly after a while. May patience, search and trust have their perfect work until the wisdom and glory of hidden things are fully revealed. In Jesus' name. Amen."

Eddie Little was at the Chapel for the special commemorative service just as he was present for many years as the first and only Sexton for the Chapel. Eddie had come to Palm Beach in 1957 from south Georgia and went to work at The Breakers Hotel after working for a landscape company for several years. At The Breakers he was responsible for maintaining the grounds around the Chapel and the Lotus Cottage. His daily labor brought him into close contact with Dr. Lindsay who took Eddie as a friend.

Eddie describes Dr. Lindsay as "a scholar ... who did a lot of writing of prayers and books ... a fine gentleman ... who came to the Chapel daily and always brought me a couple of donuts and coffee. He made sure that I had something to eat." Eddie recalls fondly that when Dr. Lindsay went north to Boston for the summer he always contacted The Breakers and told them that they should not "move me ... Dr. Lindsay was always sending packages and books back and I had to receive them on this end." As the minister aged, Eddie remembers driving him every Saturday to Green's Drug Store where "we'd have grilled cheese sandwiches and the best clam chowder. Saturdays and Sundays were my days with Dr. Lindsay and I enjoyed being with him. I used to stay overnight from time to time when his wife was still alive ... she was getting senile ... and when Dr. Lindsay became incapacitated I spent more time with him."

Eddie laughs when he relates one incident that is fresh in his mind concerning Dr. Lindsay. It was when the Chapel still faced Whitehall Way and Eddie had to arrive early on Sunday mornings to put out about three hundred chairs and a loudspeaker in the tree. "There was a parking lot opposite Cocoanut Row with cars parked east and west ... One day it got hot and I pulled my coat off and put it in a lady's car. I forgot about the coat and the lady went home with it ... I told Dr. Lindsay, 'You'll have to announce from the pulpit that I put my coat in some lady's car and she took it home with her ...' The following Sunday Dr. Lindsay got up in the pulpit and said, 'Eddie, my Sexton, left his coat in somebody's car ... and

Eddie Little with Chad and Christian Crandall (1997)

if you like the coat ... you can come back next Sunday and get the pants.'"

Eddie Little says that, as S e x t o n, under Dr. L i n d s a y ' s p a s t o r a t e, his duties were not so demanding. "It was my responsibility to see to it that he got to and from the Chapel and toward the later years I had to stand next to him on the pulpit. When Dr. Miller came to the Chapel the duties became more involved and then I was spending weekends with Dr. Lindsay as well."

After Easter of 1984 Dr. Miller and Marcella left the Chapel. They remained in the area for some time before returning to a church in Kentucky. At a Board meeting in early May Dr. Robert Gronlund, Chairman of the Pulpit Search Committee, reported that some progress, though slow, had been made on the pulpit search. "Letters of inquiry and nomination had been sent to approximately 100 sources; ten to fifteen names had been received from members and many had replied 'Yes' or 'No.'" Dr. Gronlund recommended that during the summer months, as much as possible, a candidate fill the pulpit. Gen. Scott brought out the fact that "the summer was not a good time to bring candidates due to low attendance."

As the search went forward, the music offering at the Chapel continued to be of the finest quality. There were recitals given by Frederick Swann and Christopher Herrick in addition to the dedicatory concert by Mr. Thomas on March 4th, as well as other concerts by the Director of Music.

However, the acrimony did not abate and something to rally

Dr. John and Marcella Miller

around was a welcome diversion. Sea Gull Cottage returned from the ocean to the lakeside property, to where her journey had first begun as McCormick's home in the late 1800s.

ℛETURN OF SEA GULL AND A NEW MINISTER

The Board met in the small Chapel May 1, 1984. Bob Kirkpatrick presided. Hank McCall was present as was Marshall McDonald who had returned to the area in '81. Bill Tell was in attendance as well as Irene Glass. According to the Minutes:

> "President Kirkpatrick reported interest in buying the manse resulting in an appraisal being made by James Branch in the amount of $150,000. Appraisal showed the house built in approximately 1925.
>
> President Kirkpatrick called upon Irene Glass for progress report on Sea Gull Cottage. She stated that the Preservation Foundation had asked if we would veer from the agenda sent us - that the piers (some 40 plus) be duplicated exactly, put in place and the building

then jacked up and placed on them ... The roof on the Cottage was brought to attention of J. K. Wherry... Mrs. Glass advised that the roof had been discussed, that she had been advised by the structural engineer that the roof was alright. However, it might not be after moving. It was agreed that the President and Mrs. Glass would bring up the question to Polly Earl ... Mrs. Glass reported that the Preservation Foundation formed a ceremonial committee and wanted to have a Sea Gull Cottage Day ... possibly the second week of June or the 4th of July ... President advised that we needed a Music Committee, that Hugh Pierce would like to be put on it and, in fact, would like to be Chairman. Hank McCall suggested a Mr. Arthur McCoy, who he understands has a music PhD. Lengthy discussion followed regarding music, loudness of organ, etc ... The subject of wedding fees was introduced ... Alicia Engel had been appointed wedding coordinator. She had handled three weddings and was paid no fee for her services. MOTION made by Marshall McDonald that fees for weddings be increased as follows:

Main Sanctuary $500. Small Chapel $400, Outside under tree $450...Irene Glass reported that John Floyd advised her that Dr. Lindsay would like to see 'The Flagler Memorial' again used under the name of the Chapel. William Tell saw no reason to memorialize Flagler and felt that Flagler's portrait should be placed on the east wall and Dr. George Morgan Ward's should be placed on the northwest wall."

It is of note that Flagler was not to be memorialized by some members. However, it is significant that the Cottage, Flagler's first home on the Island, be saved from demolition. It would be prophetic to return the old Cottage to within the shadows of the Royal Poinciana Hotel site from where the "Great Man" watched the building of the first Chapel in 1897-98, a smaller version, but the spiritual genesis of The Royal Poinciana Chapel that we know today. It is impossible to sit within the Chapel and not feel the very presence of Henry Flagler, the man who provided the vision and financial means to initiate the development of Palm Beach as one of the premier and richly guarded enclaves in the world today.

Polly Earl

MORT KAYE STUDIOS

It was cause for celebration then, when Sea Gull was moved to the present site on May 10, 1984. The complicated procedure was placed in the capable hands of Mr. Lindley Hoffman, engaged as architect and Polly Anne Earl, who provided leadership for the Preservation Foundation. Mr. Mike Adair of LaPlant Adair was contracted to move the building. Greg Podkulski was in charge of the severing of the Cottage and demolishing the add-on servants quarters. He declared, "She's in pretty good shape, considering she's a hundred years old. The termites have been feasting, but they didn't touch the beams or structure."

Excerpts from a brief history of the Cottage by Irene Glass provides a colorful account of the actual move:

> "The Victorian Grand Dame of Palm Beach is pushing her 100th birthday and what a proud lady she is: Originally dubbed 'Croton Cottage' because of so many crotons surrounding it, a picture of the Cottage theoretically was shown to Henry Flagler in 1892. When Flagler saw the photos, he got in a boat and went to Palm Beach to look at what Mr. McCormick, of Denver,

had built in 1886 ... and paid $35,000 for, including 50 acres of land. (Flagler) liked what he saw and paid McCormick $75,000 for the package. He lived there until 1902 when Whitehall was finished.

The great lady then became rental property for the railroad and eventually (in 1913) was moved north of The Breakers facing the ocean. It had termites, a nondescript big addition, and needed tender loving care when a group of us learned we might have the privilege of 'resurrecting' it. We knew if it were to be usable, we might want a kitchen and as we looked at it, we saw the advantage of using a seven foot wide strip of the wraparound screened porch, which idea delighted us.

After the decision was finalized to bring the painted lady back from the ocean to the circular parking lot at The Royal Poinciana Chapel, the addition was destroyed, the house was cut in two crosswise and plans were laid to 'bring her home.' It was decided to move it at night with less traffic and with Florida Power and Light lifting the electrical wires.

The two sections were put on 36 rubber tires, two conveyances, and with TV cameras and newsmen ready, it lurched forward and began its journey westward. Creaking made us gasp and there were many people walking alongside. It was pouring rain and the estimated move cost $100,000."

Eddie Little recalls that they "brought the Cottage from the ocean to County Road and then down a piece to about the fifth or sixth fairway, close to Bethesda, and then across the golf course to Cocoanut Row. It was damaging to the fairway but that was all taken care of."

According to the Glass history, the cost and magnitude of the move:

"... made lots of us wonder??? about our sanity but were sustained by the words of Ambassador Smith,

'This house is too important to become a memory.' The caravan came right through the golf course and lumbered along very slowly like an elephant with a sore foot. The movers ran back and forth and it was said that the weight was 100 tons. Against the sky, the two sections looked horrendous.

The movers paused at Cocoanut Row to check passage through bushes and the wires and one section slowly followed the other into the church parking lot. A cheer went up and an open carton of milk on an I-beam had never spilled a drop on the journey.

Then it was moved onto the foundation and the restoration began."

With the cottage "back where it belongs" the business of running the church was ever at the forefront. There was no full-time preacher but many came, one per Sunday. In August, The Reverend Dr. Thomas W. Kirkman spoke at the Chapel as the Committee continued searching for Dr. Miller's replacement.

Dr. Kirkman remembers, "We had been at Royal Oak (Michigan) for thirty years. Where had the time gone? We could account for every year but they had passed swiftly. There were not many wasted motions, and there were many wonderful achievements. However, I must admit that the demands were beginning to take more energy. I couldn't remember a time except for vacations when I didn't have counseling appointments ... it got to where I had a calendar full every night and never quite managed to get home by ten. The schedule was constant Monday through Friday and then on Friday evening a wedding rehearsal ... I was preaching three services every Sunday and there were weddings on Saturday ... I was prime for what came out of the blue. David Knox, the Mayor of Huntington Woods, a member of our congregation who had retired to Florida and was a member of the Royal Poinciana Chapel, recommended they contact me."

Dr. Kirkman's recollection continues, "A letter came explaining they were seeking someone between the ages of forty-five and fifty-five. My reply was, "I can take care of most of the criteria in the dossier but I am sixty-two, about to be sixty-three and you don't want anybody over fifty-five. They flew me down to Palm Beach to preach in August. My first contacts at the Chapel, members of the Search Committee, were Bob Kirkpatrick, Hugh Pierce, Mrs. Bea Tinsley, Barbara Pearson and Marshall McDonald. Everyone was gracious and welcoming. Dr. Lindsay was in church on that occasion, in a wheelchair with Bob Murray accompanying him. The doctor wore a special hearing aid and I could hear it clicking on and off. It was my practice at Royal Oak before the Pastoral Prayer, to have a period of silent prayer. I, therefore, announced to the congregation that we would have a few minutes of silent prayer. I soon heard Dr. Lindsay, 'The PA is off ... the PA isn't working ...' and then Bob Murray, speaking to his elderly companion in a stage whisper, 'Dr. Lindsay ... it's SILENT PRAYER' to which the old Scot loudly replied, 'I CAN'T HEAR THE SILENT PRAYER!' "

In November of 1984 Dr. Kirkman returned to Palm Beach and was called to serve at the Chapel, although he didn't preach on that occasion. He returned to Royal Oak to gather his wife Ruth, and to leave behind what had been an illustrious career, for the next pastorate, one that he thought would be less demanding. Little did he know what was ahead.

Dr. Kirkman had graduated from the University of Pennsylvania before entering Princeton Seminary. He met Ruth Kolthoff at Princeton where they were both studying for a Theological Degree. Ruth was one of the first women to be so honored as a full-time female student, graduating a year after Tom's ordination in April 1946. Ruth went off for a year on fellowship to study at the American School of Oriental Research in Jerusalem, while Tom took the position of Assistant to Dr. Irving Adams West at the House of Hope Presbyterian Church in St. Paul, Minnesota.

The House of Hope Church was not unlike Bethesda in its wealth and grandeur. During Tom's years there the membership increased by five hundred each year. The cut-stone sanctuary with magnificent stained glass windows stood quite apart from Tom's next pastorate, the Hammond Avenue Presbyterian Church in Superior, Wisconsin, where reality set in quickly. At one of the first session meetings young Tom was shocked and dismayed by a motion, "Bills will be paid if and when funds become available." The blue-collar city on the shore of Lake Superior, felt the frigid clime likened to Bemidji or International Falls, both touted as the coldest locales in the United States in winter. Tom says there was a saying, "The snow at Thanksgiving would still be there at Easter." For a girl from Miami, Ruth felt like Tom was taking her further north with every pastorate and wondered if the next move might be Alaska.

Tom found that the city with a reputation for having the highest per capita consumption of alcohol, at that time, also created a need for AA and many evenings were spent counseling the families of alcoholics. Tom relates a natural reaction to such an atmosphere: "A Mrs. Brace, member of the church and leader of the Women's Christian Temperance Union, approached me asking, 'Tom, is it true that Jesus turned water into wine?' I answered, 'Well, Mrs. Brace, I think it is true ... the people certainly thought it was wine.' Mrs. Brace responded, 'Are you sure it wasn't grape juice?'

'Mrs. Brace, the people of that day knew the difference between grape juice and wine.' The lady thought for a minute and then continued, 'Well, maybe that was all right for Jesus, but I don't think any more of Him for having done it!'"

After seven years Tom and Ruth Kirkman left Superior for the First Presbyterian Church of Royal Oak, Michigan where they would spend the next thirty years ministering to a growing congregation, adding to the church facilities in an ongoing building program, and developing foreign missions as well as performing spiritual outreach to the citizens of the Detroit suburb.

When the call came from Palm Beach it would be a wonderful opportunity to return Ruth to the warmth of the tropics. And, the benefit to the Chapel was to have two gifted theologians for the price of one.

$\mathcal{T}$HOMAS WILLIAM KIRKMAN
AND RUTH

Dr. Kirkman arrived at a time when the politics of the Chapel had created an enormous division within the membership, where intense emotions and divergent allegiances were at fever pitch. The ongoing fray had to be explained to the new minister — forewarned by Bob Kirkpatrick, "I must be honest with you. You are giving up a successful church where you are held in high esteem. The Chapel faces serious problems. It could even cease to be an ongoing institution. I don't want you to ever feel that we have misrepresented our situation."

When the problems did not abate, Bob Kirkpatrick resigned from the Presidency of the Board. His doctor advised leaving before his health suffered. It was to this travail that Dr. Kirkman came to Palm Beach.

Tom Kirkman remembers an early experience at the Chapel, "The Sunday before I preached, I sat as a member of the congregation and one of the ushers came over and said that I had to move because I was seated in a seat reserved for a member who may or may not attend service. I thought at the time that that was an interesting approach particularly when there were not more than two hundred people present. I decided a seating policy was needed."

Another early learning experience came when the Kirkmans hoped to continue their support of the Chiang Mai Mission Board, providing education and medical care to many Christians in Thailand. They edited and mailed thousands of newsletters seeking funding for the outreach program and broached the subject of benevolence to the officers of the Chapel. The rejoinder was a revelation to Tom, "We don't give them (benevolences) ... we expect them to come to us ... we're a mission church in Palm Beach."

Dr. Kirkman had occasion to speak to Dr. Lindsay on two occasions but knew from all that he heard and read that the Scottish preacher was held in high esteem and was leaving an unprecedented and rich legacy.

Before the old gentleman passed away, it had been Sam Lindsay's desire to preach at the Chapel on his hundredth birthday. He missed the opportunity by half a year. Dr. Kirkman recalls, "One of my early duties (at the Chapel) was to conduct Dr. Lindsay's funeral. I had come in January and presided over the funeral in March of 1985. I ... learned how special had been his ministry ... there were sermons and other writings by Dr. Lindsay that I found inspiring and there were accolades by the parishioners that spoke eloquently of his service to the church and to the community."

Two people eulogized the minister. Dr. Warren was one and Marjorie Whittemore was the other. Marjorie recalls, "It was not difficult to talk about one who was so special; however, it was at the same time heartbreaking because I loved Sam Lindsay and held him as one of the dearest people that I had ever known ... he meant so much to our family ... he was a very special angel." Hank McCall remembers that Marjorie spoke with such devotion in an emotional delivery that could not have been more touching.

Marilyn Polete, "Virgin Mary", would miss Dr. Lindsay. She had been his companion for years. She had watched lovingly over the aging couple and remembered that Nell was still driving as they made their way north for the summer at Lake Placid in spite of suffering the beginning stages of Alzheimers. "Nell drove to the market but often forgot where she'd put the car and the town police rescued her ... everyone knew who she was." There were many medical emergencies due to falls and visits to the doctors became routine. Marilyn was devoted to the couple and often invited them for holiday dinners. She was like a daughter to Dr. Lindsay when he lost Nell and theirs was a very special relationship until the minister passed away.

Louise Gillett also remembered Dr. Lindsay with fondness. Louise, Marilyn's mother, came to work at the Chapel part time, when Marilyn was pulled away from her duties to give personal assistance to Dr. Lindsay and Nell as the aging process took its toll. Louise remembered working in the offices in the Chapel before the Cottage was moved, when she and Marilyn were cramped for space, "our desks were butted together and we were doing a lot of work on antiquated equipment... the copy machine or the electric typewriter was always breaking down." She has vivid memories of working with Dr. Miller and with Dr. Kirkman and Ruth in the second floor offices of Sea Gull where the business of the Chapel was conducted in 'Flagler's bedroom.' She relates that Dr. Lindsay was "the most devout person I had ever met. He readily confessed to me that he was a 'Jesus man' and when I asked him, 'what would you do if you didn't have a church', his answer was without hesitation, 'Louise, I'd stand on the corner and preach.'"

It was with obvious love and a sense of humor that Louise recalls Dr. Lindsay's cunningness. "Whenever anyone came into the office to visit ... Dr. Lindsay would hear them out and when they left he never failed to exclaim, knowing they were within earshot but pretending they were out of range, 'isn't she a wonderful woman' or 'isn't he a fine man.' And when frequent requests were received to purchase the coveted Chapel membership roster, he denied relinquishing it proclaiming, 'I want to shear my own sheep.'"

Dr. Lindsay's ashes, as well as Nell's, were buried under the coconut trees entwined on the lakefront behind the Chapel. The revered minister's role at the Chapel, as in life, had left a legacy of practicing what he preached every day - a living testimony.

Dr. Kirkman, with Ruth by his side, would pick up the reins so ably held and directed for thirty years by Dr. Lindsay.

Ruth had raised her children, daughters Ellen and Carol and son, Tom III, and was fully prepared to become a vital force, along with Tom, at the Chapel. However, neither knew the background music that preceded their arrival. The discordance would be a sad revelation and a challenge to overcome.

Ruth had directed the daily vacation church school at Royal Oak. She wrote the communicants class material and for fifteen years, with assistants, had led the class of thirty to fifty ninth graders. She had taught adult Bible studies and attended women's groups, art studies, and couples' clubs and was helpful critic and editor of Tom's sermons. According to Tom, "A psychologist who had been a member of our church once said, 'In my judgment, Ruth's greatest contribution is that she is a model for the young women of the congregation. She is not afraid to confront you when you are wrong. She is her own person. The women of tomorrow will not be content to accept an authoritarian husband. You and Ruth have set the model that many of these young people do not see in their own homes, but which they will need for a successful marriage.'"

Ruth and Tom had shared the gratifying success of outreach programs established at Royal Oak. One long term mission project was the Chiang Mai Mission Board serving the northern city in Thailand that is ninety-eight percent Buddhist. They were instrumental in raising over four million dollars to build a new campus for Payap College, including a Chapel and building for the faculty of Theology.

While Ruth continued sending the newsletter seeking ongoing support for the Thai mission, Tom became engrossed in the work at the Chapel. It was during this period when Marjorie Whittemore was asked to serve on the Board of Trustees, a position held by her mother. She reports, "I was asked to take mother's place … I served for a couple of years but the turmoil in the church at that time was so totally upsetting and all I could think was that Dr. Lindsay would not have approved of the arguing and allegations."

In Tom's opinion, "The Chapel had to change if it were to survive. To a large extent, the congregation was made up of individuals who came to Florida for a week or a month or a season. The result was that the visitors saw each other as people passing by. Dr. Lindsay, the beloved former pastor, called the Chapel, 'a service station on the highway of life.' You do not have a sense of kinship with people you happen to meet at a filling station. The Christian Church is the family of God, and the members of the family have to know and respect each other. My first goal was that the Chapel should become a spiritual home where people realize that they belong to God's family and where they are strengthened in their faith. I believe the words of the hymn:

> Blessed be the tie that binds
> Our hearts in Christian love;
> The fellowship of kindred minds
> Is like to that above.

The Chapel members needed to experience the reality that they were God's family."

Marilyn Polete explains, "There was a year when the Chapel was without a minister. Before Dr. Kirkman came, it was a parade of candidates for the pulpit and amazing that for that long period of time the church held together and remained a viable, spiritual entity on the island in spite of all the travail." According to Hank McCall, "Bill and Virginia Tell hosted luncheons at the Beach Club and other members seemed in a party mode - hosting the most wonderful gatherings in their homes. The esprit de corps certainly helped hold the Chapel together."

Another dramatic change on the island certainly affected attendance at the Chapel. When The Breakers Hotel changed from a residence hotel to a convention hotel, the hundred seats reserved for hotel guests were not needed nor were they fully used. The days of the Chapel representing a "Preaching Station on the highway of Life" during the season were behind and with year round attendance, it was going to be Dr. Kirkman's challenge to fill the sanctuary as it was once filled to overflowing by Dr. Lindsay.

Don Carmichael began attending the Chapel at the same time that Dr. Kirkman became minister. Don remembers the Mai Pen Rai sermon, given at a propitious time. The inclusion of excerpts gives an example of Dr. Kirkman's style:

"One guidebook describes the Thai people this way:
Thais believe that losing your temper
is the height of bad manners.
Losing your temper achieves absolutely nothing.
If you are involved in a dispute,
you should remain calm and never shout,
no matter how much you may feel justified.
A cool head and a smile
will achieve far more
than an expression of outrage.
These words explain why the Thai people
seem to live such happy, easy-going lives.
Mai Pen Rai brings together a number of English expressions:
'It isn't important,'
'Don't sweat the small stuff,'
'Forget it,'
'Don't lose any sleep over it,'
'It's not a federal case.'"

The sermon was timely then just as it is today. The lengthy period of unrest was beginning to fade. However, there was much work to be done.

Dr. Kirkman recalls the early period at the Chapel and compares his duties with that of Royal Oak, "I left a staff of eighteen. There was much work that never came to my desk but was accomplished by assistants. At the Chapel I was 'one' and along with the board and the able assistance of Mary (Marilyn Polete), I was involved in all decision-making."

There was a need for bylaws. "Since the Chapel was inter-denominational, it was suggested that we avoid names typical of other denominations - titles like elder, deacon, trustee. Instead we used words like manager and director. I prepared the original draft of the bylaws. Hank McCall gives credit, "Using Dr. Kirkman's experience and suggestions, the by-laws set up three boards to govern and guide the Chapel. The Board of Directors, consisting of seven members, was given authority to enact recommendations, enter contracts, and to control financial obligations and expenditures.

A Board of Spiritual Managers, consisting of eighteen members divided into three classes of succeeding years, was to study and suggest policy on music, ushers, format of services, and any matters of religious nature.

A Board of Temporal Managers, with members as in the Spiritual Board, was to study and suggest policy on the building, grounds, machinery, and any physical aspects of the Chapel. Only the Board of Directors had the authority to transact business and control finances." "William Tell and Hugh Pierce used Tom's document, seeking to put their interpretation upon it." In Tom's opinion, "Bill Tell prevailed, and history has justified his judgment." The by-laws originally written by Dr. Kirkman, with Bill Tell's input, continue to direct the business of running the Chapel.

Turmoil and responsibility weighed heavily upon the new minister who sought the warmth of the Florida sun and a less arduous ministry. However, what he discovered was in sharp contrast to what he envisioned and a leisure activity was welcome. It was Don Carmichael who initiated a return to the past — an activity that took Tom from the rough waters of the Chapel to the waters of Lake Mangonia. Don recalls, "I was rowing then as a member of the Rowing Club ... when I learned that Tom had been a member of the lightweight crew at Penn I suggested he come row with me. His rejoinder, 'well, I haven't rowed in forty years', was unacceptable and I invited him out and he got into the shell and it was as if it had been just minutes before that he'd rowed at Penn ... he was gone. He took to the oars with strength and ability that just floored me ... in recounting what I had witnessed on the lake that day I facetiously said that his prowess was 'disgusting!'"

Dr. Kirkman's first major order of business was Sea Gull Cottage. He worked along with the Preservation Foundation under the guidance of Polly Earl and Earl E. T. Smith, whose contribution is summarized by Hank McCall, "He (Earl Smith) was on the board under Dr. Lindsay for many years ... He never said anything until the last remark, and then Dr. Lindsay would go the way Earl Smith suggested. He was the greatest man for saying nothing and then getting his way that I've ever run into. He was mayor of the town for many years. As a young man he stayed at the Sea Gull Cottage ... It took him a year to persuade the Chapel to let them use this land ... He said, 'I'll pay for it.' And he did pay for it ... He went in front of the Town Council, and remember, it took five years to get permission to move the Chapel and in one hour, Earl E. T. Smith had permission to move the Sea Gull Cottage from half a mile away to here."

Hank McCall wrote a "Short History of Sea Gull Cottage" that describes some of what went on after the cottage was returned to the lakeside property:

"As work progressed on Sea Gull there was much discussed. Layers of paint a quarter of an inch thick were stripped off the exterior planking. Various coats of white (Flagler Systems), yellow (Henry Flagler) and blue-gray (Robert McCormick) were revealed. Today's gray approximates the original color.

During the months of construction, there were endless discussions and arguments between the boards of the Chapel and the Preservation Foundation. It was agreed that the Chapel would buy the building and maintain it until the year 2010. After that, the Chapel could continue to use the Cottage or they could give the Preservation Foundation a year in which to move it to another location.

The question of "Landmarking" became a battle because the Chapel strongly opposed the restrictions implied by the designation. This contention was settled on June 12, 1985, when the Town Council unanimously approved designation of Sea Gull Cottage as an historical landmark but exempted the land on which the building rested.

Costs kept mounting. The Chapel paid for items like the air conditioning and kitchen, but the restoration costs exceeded $600,000, far above the $300,000 estimate. Mr. Smith never complained. He said that he would pay for it and he did, smiling as the charm of Sea Gull began to reappear."

According to Irene Glass's handwritten history of Sea Gull,

"Old photos were used for guides. We were delighted when Polly Earl, of the Preservation Foundation, found an almost identical chandelier as shown in the pictures for the West Room.

The sphinx chandelier in the Blue Room matched the sphinxes in the wallpaper. In an effort to keep within the church's budget for things ... some of the trades people donated their services ... tile setter, Ken Stephens and wallpaper hanger, John Oberg were examples. The only time the wallpaper hanger had was Sunday morning so I met him there. We locked ourselves in to avoid criticism of working on Sunday and he pasted and I cut out the pieces of wallpaper for the Gold Room ceiling. The wallpaper was specially made by Bradbury & Bradbury in California. They later came and showed us a video about the wallpaper.

The fish scale shingles on the outside were a delight. Blue ceilings as signs of the times in the porches were a must. The original marble is in the foyer.

When the many, many layers of paint were pulled

off the newel post, the paint stood alone. Beneath was the carved newel post we have today. The other newel post had to be made and carved as the original one was not usable.

A beautiful lozenge in the center of the wood floor is to be found in the northwest room upstairs.

Through the generosity of a church lady we put the Flagler rose in the glass doors of the kitchen cabinets.

The spandrels, stained glass and gilded strip moldings were all shown in the photos.

Over $600,000 was paid by the Preservation Foundation of Palm Beach for the restoration of this 'working landmark.'"

Another brief paper regarding the Cottage lists some of its amenities - some authentic, others reproductions:

"The main entrance hall holds original marble and woodwork and an Eastlake style hall mirror. The South Room or the original dining room has Jamaica shutters after original window treatments, the wallpaper after Christopher and a dresser to complement antique neo-Egyptian chandelier. The North Room which was the original library is done in neo-classical wallpaper borders and the room was enlarged in 1897. Over the door is a transom of original kokomo glass from Brelsford House. The Main Parlor, the showpiece of the restoration has five different wallpaper designs typical of the Victorian Era, the furniture donated by the Colonial Dames of America, Chapter 17, wallpaper typical of the aesthetic, Eastlake and Anglo-Japanese styles combined in an eclectic manner - original woodwork in the Eastlake style on fireplace - chandelier an almost exact replica of original - antique and reproduction spandrels - gilt strips on walls as in original pictures.

The Main Stair is of mahogany timbers from shipwreck and originally terminated in third story tower, now demolished.

East Stairway chandelier from Bradley's Beach Club
- leaded window from Brelsford House."

And then from a report dated August - September 1986
of the Preservation Foundation entitled: "SEA GULL
HONORED"

MORT KAYE STUDIOS

Earl T. Smith and wife Leslie

"Ambassador Earl E. T. Smith, Chairman of the Preservation Foundation of Palm Beach, Inc., is pleased to announce that Sea Gull Cottage has received two awards from the Florida Trust for Historic Preservation. The awards, one for Outstanding Preservation Project in the category of Restoration of a Residential Structure and the second in the category of Outstanding Achievement in the Restoration of Historic Interiors, mark the first time that a preservation project in the Town of Palm Beach has been so honored.

These juried awards have been presented by the Florida Trust for Historic Preservation since 1982. This year the Florida Trust considered sixty different submissions from all areas of the state for the awards. Only one other structure in Palm Beach County, the Boca Raton Town Hall, has won a Florida Trust award.

The Preservation Foundation of Palm Beach wishes to acknowledge the contribution of its restoration architect, Lindley Hoffman, A.I.A., of Hoffman Schofield Colgan Architects. We also wish to thank Mrs. Philip N. Fortin; the Colonial Dames of America, Chapter 17; the Daughters of the American Revolution, Palm Beach Chapter; and the Garden Club of Palm Beach for their contribution to the Sea Gull Restoration. The Florida Trust awards will be presented formally by Secretary of State, George Firestone, at the annual meeting of the Florida Trust in Fort Lauderdale, September 27th.

Erna Ross on right with neice Esther Moller

SEA GULL TRANSFERRED TO CHAPEL

On Sunday, September 14th, 1986, at the Royal Poinciana Chapel, the Preservation Foundation completed the formal transfer of Sea Gull Cottage to the Royal Poinciana Chapel. (The purchase price was paid by one 1886 silver dollar). As provided by our original agreement with the Chapel, the Chapel will now assume the responsibility for maintaining Sea Gull in its historic appearance.

The Chapel will use Sea Gull for its parish activities. The Preservation Foundation headquarters remain open to all members on the second floor of Sea Gull."

There was more to celebrate. Another event, in 1987 albeit not to rival the official transfer of Sea Gull, or even particularly pertinent to the Chapel history, but newsworthy enough to warrant inclusion in the Guinness Book of Records. Chapel member, Erna Ross, who would live to be 104 years of age and enjoyed the game of golf almost until the end of her life, at 97, had a hole in one at The Everglades Club. When asked what club she used, Erna assuredly answered, "My driver, of course!"

Sea Gull 'Croton' Cottage

ℛENEWAL AND EXPANSION

Dr. Kirkman's arrival did not immediately quell the upheaval. The acrimony enveloped him in spite of a noble attempt to bring peace and forgiveness to the Chapel. Bob Kirkpatrick, under doctor's orders, resigned as President of the Board and Bill Tell was elected to fill the vacancy. Emotions were at fever pitch and there continued to be a fall-out in membership.

Barbara Pearson had been a regular member of the quartet as well as soloist at the Chapel for years. At the centennial celebration in '84, commemorating Reverend Dilley's 'Lake Worth Union Congregational Church' from which the Chapel evolved, Barbara sang along with Glen D. Arfsten, Tenor, Marijane Elliott, Contralto and Clarence Smith, Baritone, in what was a continuing stellar performance of the highest quality as per Henry Flagler's behest.

Barbara's music training had begun at the age of six as a piano student of Marie Gillet of the New England Conservatory. At thirteen she changed her focus to voice which she pursued in music, cum laude, from Tufts University. She was an Adjunct Professor of Voice at the Hartt School in Hartford and when she came to Palm Beach, taught at Palm Beach Atlantic College.

When Barbara married Ray Johnson in

Barbara Pearson Johnson

1987, Dr. Kirkman performed the wedding ceremony in the Chapel and Thomas Thomas provided the organ accompaniment. The two musicians held the utmost respect for one another. It was sad, then, when Thomas Thomas submitted his resignation in 1988.

A new Minister of Music was sought. Dr. Jack W. Jones was hired and brought a rich musical heritage to the Chapel having received a Bachelor of Music Degree from Stetson University, a Master of Sacred Music Degree from Union Theological Seminary and a Doctor of Musical Arts Degree from the Juilliard School. While studying in New York, Jack served as accompanist for many vocal studios and was teaching assistant to musicologist Gustave Reese. His early career included the prestigious title of Organist-Director of Music Activities for the United States Military Academy at West Point and Associate Organist-Choirmaster of The Cathedral Church of St. John The Divine in Manhattan. When he came to Palm Beach he served as Music Director at the Methodist Church as well as at the First Baptist Church. He was Founder-Director of The Masterworks Chorus in addition to being Artistic Director of The Gilbert & Sullivan Light Opera Society. His commitment to the cultural scene on the Island would serve the Chapel well.

When Barbara Johnson decided to retire from performing as vocalist, she devoted her musical talents to accompaniment as pianist occasionally playing at the Sunday worship service as well as in concert with Jack Jones. Barbara credits Jack with his "marvelous attention to detail and organization ... he has the complete music program laid out with every hymn, prelude, solo and choral introit determined a year in advance."

Dr. Jack Jones

MORT KAYE STUDIOS

What a blessed church did Henry Flagler found, the doors open to one and all in a true celebration of ecumenism, promoting world-wide Christian unity.

However, the old church had been moved from place to place and was badly in need of refurbishing. Fortunately, in spite of the emotional tumult, there were many talented and distinguished individuals willing to come forward and serve the needs of the Chapel. Restoring it to former simple elegance would help ameliorate the hurt and unify the members of the Little White Church by the Trail.

Don Carmichael was Treasurer in 1988 when the Chapel Restoration was performed. In a bulletin to introduce the proposed renovation the following details are of interest:

"The Royal Poinciana Chapel building was moved to its present location in 1972-73. Except for the installation of the organ in 1984, no significant change or improvement has been made in the sixteen years in which the Chapel has stood on its present location.

The seats were purchased secondhand in 1900, 1910, and 1923 and are now beyond repair. The carpet has seen sixteen years of wear and is torn, frayed, and soiled. Major improvements in lighting and sound systems, unavailable in 1973, should now be installed. The painting of the Chapel will continue the present color scheme. The painting of the interior, the refurbishing of the lavatories, and the reworking of the speaker's platform are included in the planned renovation.

A renovation committee, selected from members of the boards of the Chapel, has been meeting for well over a year to study the best solution to these problems. The congregation voted without dissent to secure the necessary $200,000 and proceed with the renovation.

Considerable study was given to the seating. Padded theatre seats would cost well over $100,000. Pews padded on the seats and the backs will cost $43,000. Your Directors believe that modern theatre seats are not appropriate. The majority of the congregation favor pews. A contract has been let to the Sauder Company for pews.

Many hours of study were given to the floor. Three choices were given serious consideration. Some suggested a slate floor, others believed that a wood floor would be more suitable. The Directors decided to use an oak floor. The floor in the Chapel was wood for most of the Chapel's history. Carpeting of the main aisle and platform area is under consideration.

The lighting and the electrical system of the Chapel

do not meet the needs of evening services, weddings, and concerts. The sound system is in need of replacement. This will include hearing assistance devices which will allow the worshippers to sit anywhere in the Chapel and still enjoy the advantages of a hearing device.

St. Edward's Church has agreed to allow the Chapel to use their Parish House during the period required for renovation.

It has been the past policy of the Chapel to have the necessary funds prior to capital improvements. It is our desire to continue that policy.

Financial planning is an important aspect of the plan. If you have not given to the Restoration Fund or made a pledge for this project, we invite you to use the form to indicate your participation in the restoration of the Chapel."

It was upon completion of the refurbishing of the sanctuary when Dr. Kirkman, having read through papers and agreements in order to get "some sort of historical perspective on the Chapel", went to the Board of Directors and asked, "Do you want a Columbarium?" When he explained, "a Columbarium is a structure of vaults to hold cinerary urns", they approved the idea. Upon approval, Tom said, "It was too previous to consider building where the Cottage stands, so the present location was chosen and the type of Columbarium was also agreed upon. We decided against the design where ashes are co-mingled and designed the building to provide room for a like structure to be added in the future."

As in every request for support, a brochure was produced describing the Columbarium. The front cover held a graphic of a tree and the title:

"THE TREE OF LIFE:

A TRADITION

To him that overcometh will I give to eat of the tree of life, which is in the midst of the paradise of God. Rev. 2:7

THE COLUMBARIUM"

An explanation within the brochure is headed:

"OUR CHRISTIAN TRADITION

The Christian's hope in life and death is centered in the resurrection of Jesus Christ. Easter is the most important celebration of the Christian year. It reminds us that death is the golden gate to eternal life.

Columbarium

Because our faith gives us hope in the face of death, it is natural that Christians should wish to be buried close to the place associated with their faith. The early Christians buried within the church itself. Westminster Abbey is the final resting place of many of England's leaders.

Because the space in church buildings is limited, the churchyard cemetery came into use. Only in recent times have cemeteries been the common place of burial. A columbarium on Chapel ground is a return to the faith and practice of the early Christian church and a witness to our faith in the resurrection.

A columbarium is an area or building for the burial of ashes of the deceased. It is an appropriate and dignified resting place, wholly in accord with the Christian faith."

The brochure held a sketch of the proposed building as well as a small map showing the site plan including the Chapel and Sea Gull Cottage.

The Columbarium, according to Don Carmichael, cost approximately $150,000. Before the Columbarium was built, Don knew that, "in view of the planned expansion, it was necessary to take into consideration the area required so that we should not mislocate the Columbarium or place it in conflict with future expansion."

Tom Kirkman recalls, "We had outgrown Sea Gull Cottage. A new building providing a fellowship hall and new offices was going to be a costly and major undertaking. In placing the Columbarium, we had to keep in mind that when the twenty-five year agreement with the Preservation Foundation terminated, in 2015, use of the property can be formulated. Hopefully there will be funding at that time to move the Cottage. The property would be ideal for a private school for island young people. For the time being it serves the Chapel well for Sunday School and for other special functions."

In November 1990, Marshall McDonald was President of the Board of Directors when the Board of Temporal Managers requested that a study be made for increased space for the administration of the Chapel. Don Carmichael was a member of the Board and recalls, "We had set up a Long Range Planning Committee under the direction of Dr. Trudy Couch. I studied the growth in terms of membership and attendance and projected out, each year, determining that the facilities were not going to be adequate to meet our needs five years down the line. My report to Trudy and the committee set the ball rolling and for months they analyzed what the needs would be as we approached the next millennium. The plan called for so many square feet for office space, so much for fellow-

PAST PRESIDENTS OF THE BOARD

Edmund Taylor 1957-1960

Alvin Boettcher 1964-1966

Richard Scott 1975-1976

William Tell 1977-1979, 1986-1988

H. Clarence McCall 1980-1983

Robert Kirkpatrick 1984-1985

Marshall McDonald 1988-1990

Donald Carmichael 1991-1993

George Slaton 1993-1994

John Randolph 1994-1996

Chester Claudon 1996-1997

Charles Warwick 1997-1998

ship and kitchen, etc. It was a very detailed analysis that was presented for approval. I then took that information forward seeking an architectural firm. Bob Nichols, a member of the Chapel, was considered. Ray Wells

Mr. & Mrs. Marshall Rinker

MORT KAYE STUDIOS

along with Tom Kirkman and I studied Bob's ability to perform the work, estimated to cost a couple of million dollars. The increased area was to be ten to twelve thousand square feet of expansion. Ray Wells felt that Nichols and Associates could handle the job."

"Bob Nichols," according to Don, "worked out the preliminary plans in early '91 and we hired a local contractor to estimate what the actual cost would be including having the organ re-worked and some additional refurbishing of the sanctuary — reworking the air conditioning, etc. In the Fall of '91 we went into a fund-raising program. I was concerned about raising the money, but, happily, within three or four months, we had enough money committed to go ahead with the project. Pledges were made which was a great relief to me. 'Doc' Rinker really kicked it off by giving $500,000 and we placed a four-foot thermometer as you walked into the sanctuary letting the attendees watch the fiscal progress. What was particularly rewarding, in addition to some large pledges of fifty and sixty thousand, was the outpouring from some of the women who came to me asking, 'would you consider a contribution of $200 over three years?' That absolutely delighted me because I knew that that was a lot of money to them and they would have to give up something ... but they wanted to be a part of the expansion."

Don remembers, "We broke ground after Easter of '92. The

general contracting business was slow at the time. Weitz Company was selected as contractor and in order to keep their large staff busily engaged they gave us a very decent bid. The office space behind the sanctuary, added in the seventies, was the first to go. We were careful not to disturb any of the old portion of the sanctuary."

"What concerned me from the outset was that we needed to put up more space than was in the original sanctuary, adding twelve thousand square feet to the ten in the old building. I did not want to create something that would over-shadow the sanctuary. We wanted something of simple elegance that would continue the theme of the old 'meetinghouse.' With that in mind the arched window on the north wall of the fellowship hall is smaller than the arched window on the north wall of the sanctuary. All of what was being done had to be approved by the Landmarks Commission and we worked closely with Jane Volk and the Town of Palm Beach. There were obstacles to overcome. The stairs in the fellowship hall, for fire protection reasons, were to be closed with a fire-door. We had worked on the design of the reception area, with particular attention to flow and grace and the door would destroy that feeling. We negotiated with the Town promising to sprinkle the whole area if they would not force us to enclose the stairway. We won the battle!"

"Another detail, attempting to stay within budget, we faced having to eliminate two sets of French doors on the west side of the hall. By scrutinizing the over-all plans taking from here and giving there, we saved those doors."

"We had established a six month scheduling to be completed by the beginning of Season. When we were ready to roof, Hurricane Andrew went through Dade County and every roofer in the area and from out-of-state could make twenty dollars more an hour in the leveled portions of south Miami and Homestead. Plywood became exceedingly difficult to obtain ... fortunately a member of the Chapel had a lumber company in North Carolina and he came through with all we needed. We had it shipped down."

"During the entire project I held a construction committee

meeting every Friday with Tom prominently involved, as well as Judy Golembiewski, treasurer, who governed the cash flow in order to meet our bills as they came in. Fortunately we never had to borrow a penny - complying with the overriding dictum of Henry Flagler never to incur debt ... Judy was indispensable throughout the process."

"I had a site superintendent at the meetings and any sub-contractors that we were dealing with at the moment to obviate any problems or concerns according to the 'flow-chart.' We worked on a commitment that if the work was completed early, they received a bonus and if delayed, for any reason, a penalty was applied. Work was completed just a few weeks behind schedule but because Weitz had done such a thorough and conscientious job, the board approved not penalizing them."

"One of my main objectives through the process, was to build a team effort, avoiding an adversary arrangement between us and the contractor and we enjoyed a cooperative relationship throughout."

"There was a serious problem with the organ. We made a deposit and were ready to ship it to Möeller in Jacksonville, ignorant of the fact that they were in bankruptcy. We were within a day of loading it on a truck when we learned that another church never got their organ back. We lost the $25,000 deposit. We then called upon the representative of Reuter Organ Company who came to the Chapel and pointed out that, 'all the chambers had to be re-designed using acoustical technology.'" A letter from Chester Claudon to Don Carmichael dated October 17, 1992 gives evidence of a determined effort to ascertain a competent restoration of the organ:

"As per your request, I paid another visit to Reuter ... I clarified for them, the current situation and asked Mr. Vaughan to check my September 15 report for accuracy. He indicated the report was factual and correct, and only suggested a few additional words to further clarify ... Enclosed find the re-drafted report with the few minor word additions, but most important, and that is, the lack of a Tierce pipe."

The six page report is inclusive of many technical details to provide confidence by the Board of Trustees that indeed Reuter Organ Company, Lawrence, Kansas, was performing a wondrous restoration. The report concludes that "designated organ 5954 is being re-worked with portions of said organ in almost every segment of the plant. The large facade pipes are in the process of being cleaned and refurbished ... not part of the contract but felt that since these were the ones seen by the congregation, they should be highly polished and uniform ... Seeing the stained and discolored ones ... it certainly reinforced decision to take the pipes back ... the most striking observation was the difference between the Austin organ installed in 1982 and the much older Möeller installed in the '60s, particularly in reference to quality."

The report further mentions the cloning of copper pipes to replace the zinc pipes ... "I am convinced that the difference in timbre, etc., will not be detectable ... apparently, the original pipes were made of German zinc, and you could see where these pipes had gradually bent and warped and were not performing at full efficiency..."

Chester Claudon, who had paid all travel expenses to oversee the work in progress, was keen to observe many details. He mentions "the bottom and resonators on the English Horn" and that "Reuters has a policy to construct any reed pipe shorter than four feet in size, out of spotted metal: 50% tin and lead alloy that they actually pour and form in their own plant ... the old leather components, the Vox Humana valves (known as 'frogs') were being completely replaced ... cork replaced with leather on some of the Pitman valves ... approximately 1,000 valves ... the main air chambers and reservoirs were being rebuilt ... some were cracked and obviously leaking badly and required substantial stiffeners and all new leather ... all work done by hand or on hand operated machines."

Chester saw, "the swell louvers, refurbished and working beautifully to cover the swell, the choir and the solo pipes" and his report refers to Mr. Vaughan "showing me the largest reed pipes, 16 feet high, explaining that these were substituting for 32 foot pipes ... he indicated that you get half the tone, but you do get the same cycles per second, the same pitch." When the console was considered, it was not shipped to Reuters. In their opinion the console was in excellent condition but "we could have a significant problem with (the) double wrapped cotton cover on the wire ... the National Electrical Code will not permit the use of that wire ... they require a poly vinyl chloride insulating material ... (however) the law grandfathered installations such as this ... until such time as wiring needed to be replaced ... by code-approved wire ... replacement of all the wire could be very expensive and should be avoided ... "

James Haggerty (1988)

Through Chester's son, Vice President and Loan Officer at the United Missouri Bank in Kansas City, a credit check was run and Reuters was found to be "growing stronger with each passing month ... I saw no signs of lack of business ... the factory was clean, busy, well organized and I really think you and Charlie picked a winner with Reuter."

It was obvious from the report that in Chester Claudon, the Chapel had a wonderful advocate who gave unselfishly of his time and interest in behalf of the beloved Little White Church by the Trail.

"Upon completion of the extensive work we then had an instrument, an Austin Opus 2685, that incorporated all of the former Möeller pipework and includes 58 new ranks of Austin pipes. It is one of the finest organs in Florida, truly worthy of Flagler's Church."

Don was generous with well deserved accolades, "one of the

Building of Kirkman Hall

key people in the building of the fellowship hall was Jim Haggerty who had had experience as a superintendent in maintenance before retiring. Jim was good about looking over details. In one instance a water system was hooked up incorrectly and there were other errors where retro-fitting would have been costly. His scrutiny was invaluable."

While the building project was in progress, Sea Gull Cottage continued providing a place for church school and for the many other activities associated with the church. According to Hank McCall's history of Sea Gull, "What happy days Sea Gull brought to the Chapel! Church fellowship hours, potluck suppers, lawn parties, wedding receptions, picnics, socials on the porch while watching Fourth of July fireworks and boat parades became regular events. After so many years of absence, Sunday School classes were organized for the children.

Perhaps the most joyous occasion was the hundredth birthday party given for Alice Rooke by her family. It was an 'old fashioned' ice cream party in perfect matching of Sea Gull's era. The champagne, the music, the ice cream, and the goodies brought us close to the glories of the Flagler days."

'The goodies' served in the Cottage were often there due to

Hazel Kennedy. With husband Francis, Hazel came to Palm Beach from Northbrook, a suburb of Chicago, in 1979. Hazel recalls, "We chose the Chapel because I remember riding by and admiring the precious New England type church and also because it was interdenominational. When we joined the Chapel in 1980 Dr. Lindsay was still sharing the pulpit with Dr. Miller. The hospitality after Sunday service was being administered by Alicia Engle who asked one Sunday if I would help serve ... as a matter of fact she told me that I

Kirkman Hall from the west

had to bake cookies. I then, faithfully, every Friday, baked batches of cookies until it suddenly dawned on me that I was the only one baking them ... others were bringing store-bought cookies. When Alicia decided to give up the duty she informed me that I WAS IN CHARGE."

Hazel recalled serving the goodies outside in those days before Sea Gull Cottage was moved from the ocean shore. "We served from a table set up on the lawn ... Alicia used to drag the orange juice in a refrigerated case each Sunday and also the cranberry juice because we didn't have any place to store things. Leftovers were put into the Little Chapel at the back of the church, hidden behind the piano. "When it rained, we tried to crowd everyone into the small Chapel but that wasn't satisfactory. Francis and

I used to buy everything at Costco, cases and cases of cranberry juice that we carted in the trunk of our car along with plates and cups ... then finally the church began ordering what was needed. Presently we just bring in the cookies and coffee cake and cream each week."

Hazel elaborated on the role of the hospitality committee, "On Christmas Eve we always served eggnog and punch and cookies and there was a time when we often served at the musical programs and we put out a spread after memorial services. During the Kirkman years the potluck suppers were popular and we always got there early to help Tom and Ruth set up the tables and prepare the coffee and tea ..."

When the fellowship hall was being built, Hazel wrote down suggestions for the kitchen area although she modestly informed "I'm not that great a cook ... but I knew there were some things that should be considered ... When I saw something that the architect was planning that I thought was wrong I didn't hesitate expressing my opinions ... when I walked in and saw the sink on the right I knew that wasn't good and that it should be around the corner out of sight. We knew we needed deep drawers to put cups in ... we used to put cups on shelves and you'd open the cabinet door and they came crashing out ..."

Hazel Kennedy played a significant role at the Chapel for years and her experience in the kitchen of the Cottage is reflected in a practical, well designed facility in the fellowship hall.

The new hall was dedicated as Kirkman Hall upon completion in 1993. George Slaton was President of the Board and presided over the reception attended by many Town leaders both from the secular as well as religious communities and members of the Chapel. It was an auspicious occasion marking the establishment of a facility that has been fully utilized by many different associations.

Tom and Ruth could take pleasure in the many contributions to the betterment of the Little White Church by the Trail. It had been enlarged measurably and much had been accomplished. However, Tom Kirkman and Don Carmichael, through it all, man-

Ruth and Tom Kirkman

aged to find time for rowing as a welcome exercise routine. Don reports on one occasion when they were rowing close to the thickly over-grown shoreline of Lake Mangonia, "suddenly Tom's scull disappeared in the reeds and after a few moments I called out, 'Tom, what are you doing in there?' His rejoinder was classic, 'I'm looking for Moses!'"

Dr. Kirkman credits Dr. Lindsay as instigator of the Fellowship of Christians and Jews. "Years ago Dr. Lindsay and the Reverend Hundson Cary of Bethesda, decided to hold a shared observance at Thanksgiving ... Some of my friends in the Jewish community came to me, 'Tom, we need you to become a part of this group.' At their request I did become an active participant in the expanded group that includes Leonid Feldman, Rabbi at Temple Emanu-El, The Reverend Ralph Warren of Bethesda and Father Francis Lechiara of St. Edwards ... I do believe that it is a positive and reinforcing tool to help bring people together and I have certainly been enriched by the involvement ... It's been gratifying to see people of diverse religious philosophies congregate and particularly to do so in each of the houses of worship ... Sometimes I think that psychological aspects of life are more important than intellectual ones. One does not always change his attitude or behavior by education alone but more by feeling, communication, and more fully recognizing the commonalities that exist in all mankind."

The Kirkmans found life on the island of Palm Beach quite disparate from Royal Oak, or Superior or St. Paul. Palm Beach has always attracted visitors from all over the world and the residents are quite accustomed to the eccentric and even bizarre. Never in all his career as minister had Tom performed a wedding when a dog walked down the aisle as a member of the wedding party, fully dressed in white with a flower at the shoulder.

According to Eddie Little, "When Dr. Kirkman came to the Chapel I found him to be very exacting and punctual and I liked that. He also had me performing additional duties ... I had to assemble the wedding party in a room in the back and stay with them until time for the ceremony and then lead them around to the front ... just like a wedding coordinator ... I'd give Jack Jones the signal and we'd go ahead." Eddie observed the wedding when the dog walked down the aisle, and also when the police were required to keep peace. Eddie refers to the "bad wedding" when one side of the family made threats against the other and detectives grilled him about whether or not a particular person had been seen on the premises. On another occasion Eddie was at the Chapel for a wedding rehearsal which went off smoothly. However, the following day, after what had been a routine rehearsal and dinner party the day before, word came to the Chapel, after all last minute preparations had been made, that the whole affair was canceled. And it was Tom who found himself defending his role in the wedding of Jim Sullivan to Sukki after serious allegations of murder in the Atlanta Constitution had been printed. When a reporter questioned whether or not Tom offered marital counseling, Tom handled the questioning with a depth of experience that put an end to further interrogation.

"Without the Kirkmans", according to Hank McCall, "the Chapel would not be in the splendid condition it is today. First and foremost, they were peace makers. They stepped into a battle of grand-daddy bull elephants butting heads to get their own way or simply for power. While this power struggle was raging we entered into an agreement with the Preservation Foundation to move Sea

Gull Cottage. They, too, had ivory-headed convictions that they expressed vehemently."

"Tom held his temper through every occasion, listened with sympathy, and always came up with a joke to get a laugh and to create a relaxed atmosphere."

Hank's praise continues, "Working together with the Kirkmans had a spirit of friendship and good will that slowly soothed the savages or worked around their demands. They were not only peace-makers but were team builders. Slowly they initiated weekly Bible studies and monthly potluck suppers that created a joyous companionship that spread through the congregation. Then they started an Enrichment Hour on Sunday mornings, inviting speakers who led discussions on travel, civic endeavors, local history, and incorporating unusual aspects of the Bible. While very quietly starting these activities, they worked with Don Carmichael to computerize the office, the membership and the finances. This led to monthly newsletters."

"It was Ruth who helped keep the Sunday school running. It had been approximately thirty years since the Chapel had a Sunday School. This effort brought in younger couples of great vigor and charm who, as parents, wanted Christian education for their children."

"Since Tom liked to cook, he instigated picnic cookouts for the Fourth of July fireworks, boat parades, or any other good excuse for a get-together on our lovely grounds."

"Tom's opening prayers at the Forum Club were warm and friendly and sometimes more interesting than the speaker. Tom and Ruth had a knack for business and promotion. Under their leadership extensive remodeling was accomplished to the main Chapel building, Sea Gull was moved and restored in its present location and the fellowship hall was built. In each instance all the money necessary was raised before the projects were completed. Their vision of what the Chapel should be as a year-round religious inspirational church came into being because of their practical and cheerful Christian leadership."

Ted Hepburn gives further accolades to the special qualities that he feels is the Kirkman legacy. Ted and Carole moved from Cincinnati, Ohio to Palm Beach in late 1986. Dr. Lindsay and Dr. Miller were gone. Tom and Ruth were in the middle of the turbulence that had engulfed the Chapel for some years. Ted credits Tom and Ruth with "reversing a severely negative trend in attendance and general optimism of the membership." Ted continued,

Judith A. Golembiewski

"our wonderful Chapel was in such a state of disarray ... I recall how difficult it was for Tom and Ruth. As only Tom Kirkman could handle it ... the unrest was finally settled and in a way that our wonderful Chapel benefitted." Ted served with Hank McCall on the Temporal Board and recalls, "The expansion is a perfect example of Tom's superior management skills. In my almost 50 years of work, I have never seen an executive as adept at creating a consensus on a project. The expansion was a great example of this, as was the Columbarium. Tom gently steered us into a project which would have been unthinkable a few years earlier. I was thrilled when the Board recognized this by naming the new fellowship hall KIRKMAN HALL ... In only ten short years he took the Chapel from a Spiritual Service Station, serving some part-time residents, to a full fledged, year around church. And he planned for the future by making sure we were not saddled with the messy doctrine and bureaucratic problems so many churches face. 'Bus' Reynolds and I were co-chairmen of investments for the Lindsay Fund and watched the fund assets more than double. This demonstrated firsthand how Tom could gently suggest a project and get the job done. He never looked for accolades or wanted any credit. But it was Tom who was the hidden hand behind what our Chapel is today." Ted's enthusiasm continues, "Tom's managerial talents were really second to his ability as a Preacher. I had never attended a church where the members openly discussed what the sermon meant to them when the service ended. This happened Sunday after Sunday during Tom Kirkman's era. He really knew how to communicate."

Another voice gives credence to Dr. Kirkman's business acumen. Judy Golembiewski had been attending the Chapel for some time when she decided to join soon after the Kirkman ministry began. She recalls, "It was at Thanksgiving." Judy soon became much more than a member, "It was only a year after I'd joined when I was invited to serve on the Board. Dr. Don Black, a minister from my church in Kankakee was visiting the area and informed Dr. Kirkman of my work in the Methodist Church. I was the first woman to ever serve on the Board of Trustees for the Illinois church. When Dr. Kirkman asked me to serve on the Spiritual Board I accepted and when the board convened after the Annual Meeting, they immediately elected me to the Board of Directors. It was a total surprise to me and suddenly," said with a humorous inflection, "I felt like I was on 'Flagler's Railroad' . . . being railroaded into the business of the Chapel." Judy went on to express, "when I first went on the Board Don Carmichael was Treasurer and Marshall McDonald was President. George Slaton then served as Treasurer for a year. When Don Carmichael became President I was asked to be Treasurer and I've held the office ever since. I must say that it's been a very rewarding experience, permitting me to meet and work with some wonderful people while providing a service that I felt qualified to do."

As Vice President and Trust Administrative Officer for Harris Trust Company, Judy is occupied with a full-time job but managed over the years to go to the Chapel office at least once a week to sign checks and is issued a monthly print-out of operating funds, scrutinized before she reports to the Board of Directors. "When I look back at the expansion project I wonder how Don and I managed to carve out the time required working with so many numbers during a lengthy, complicated process ... it was tremendously time-consuming but equally gratifying … a real labor of love."

While Judy may not be visibly prominent in the various ladies organizations within the Chapel, her contribution to its fiscal soundness is to be commended. Judy expresses how she worked closely with Dr. Kirkman and had such great respect and "a wonderful working relationship" with the minister who would soon turn the pulpit over to a new minister.

Anne Carmichael worked with Tom as a member of the Benevolence Committee. Anne inspired the Holiday Boutique, hostessing a luncheon at her home and presenting a proposal for ways to raise money for the benevolence program. "Lucia Childs volunteered to co-chair the boutique, offering items from her own shop in addition to items from shops on South Dixie. When the boutique derived a profit, we expanded our initial plans and with some funding available began going to a gift market and buying wholesale to sell retail. Every summer a buying trip became routine and the boutique in Sea Gull Cottage held in November became a successful fund raiser."

According to Anne, "When the fellowship hall was completed we moved the boutique to the larger facility and with the move the boutique also grew in size. We started with eighty to a hundred volunteers including those that provided home baked items for sale. It has more recently expanded to two hundred and fifty volunteers. We offered baked goods from the beginning, but the men's bake sale auction began when the fellowship hall was in use. The auction was designed to draw men into the activity. An important secondary purpose for the boutique was to engage the members of the congregation in a project where they could better know one another while working in a mutually gratifying project to raise money for various causes. The boutique has been highly successful with an enormous amount of work performed by everyone involved to make it so."

Don Carmichael shares with Anne an appraisal of Tom's role based on past experience in benevolence works and what he found when he accepted the call from the Chapel. "Tom had served in various ministries where active benevolence organizations and giving programs had been highly successful. Up to that point, in the history of the Chapel, most of the people here were seasonal and gave heavily, in many instances, to their churches up north. When they came to Palm Beach they were hounded by various charities in Palm Beach and gave to those organizations. Because of this," according to Don, "the general feeling was that people weren't interested in a benevolence program in the Chapel because they were giving substantially elsewhere. The Board of Directors were sensitive to this sentiment and, therefore, never attempted to launch any such program. When Tom arrived he recognized this resistance toward initiating any heavy programs, but felt that benevolence was an important aspect of church work and he supported Anne when she proposed the Boutique. As a matter of fact when Anne would have a year when they raised twelve or fifteen thousand dollars, she lamented the fact that it was not a good return when it took so much work from so many people. Tom's rejoinder is laudatory, 'Anne, I don't care if we don't raise a penny ... the fellowship that this activity generates is the most important aspect of the whole thing ...'"

Peace had returned to the Chapel. The sanctuary and organ were refurbished, a Columbarium graciously sits behind the new Kirkman Fellowship Hall, and Sea Gull still resides close to its original locale, its future to be determined by the Preservation Foundation. Tom's contribution to the Chapel cannot be overstated and he had served as minister for almost fifty years when he announced at the Annual Meeting on February 12, 1995 that he planned to retire. He asked that a committee be formed to search for his successor. Another chapter was about to close in the church history.

In Tom Kirkman's biography, prepared after his retirement and entitled, "Blessed On My Way", he described what, "I Believe:

> Sometime in life, every individual has to decide the basic convictions by which he will live. The Scripture rightly proclaims, 'We walk by faith and not by sight.' What we believe makes us what we are.

In my days at Princeton Seminary, I believed the Christian faith because it was logical. I could have given you a dozen proofs for the existence of God. Early in my ministry, it occurred to me that faith did not need proofs. If you can prove something, it is no longer a matter of faith. The author of the Epistle to the Hebrews defined faith. He wrote, 'To have faith is to be sure of the things we hope for, to be certain of the things we cannot see.' Briefly let me set forth the faith which I have lived and proclaimed.

I BELIEVE IN GOD. It is one thing to say that God is an omnipotent being. It is something quite different to address the Almighty, saying, 'Thou art my rock and my salvation.' God is not understood by human reasoning; He is perceived by His presence and grace.

In one sense, we can never really understand God; we cannot fully know God. God is infinite and we are finite. The finite will never really understand the Infinite. Thus we speak of God in symbols. God is the Good Shepherd, the loving Father, the Creator, the Everlasting Arms. All our symbols are imperfect descriptions of God; they are only fingers which point in the direction of the Almighty.

We believe that God manifests himself in different ways. As I am a husband to my wife, a father to my children, and a minister to my congregation, so God reveals himself to us as the Father, the Savior, and the Holy Spirit. This is not to suggest that there are three gods. It is to affirm that we experience God in three different ways.

I BELIEVE IN JESUS. I believe that Jesus was perfect man and perfect God. As much deity as can be put in humanity was resident in Jesus so that we human beings could gain an understanding of God. His life and death made divine forgiveness possible. The hymn states the proposition best:

> There was no other good enough
> To pay the price of sin,
> He only could unlock the gate
> Of heaven and let us in.

Christ did for us what we cannot do for ourselves.

I BELIEVE IN THE BIBLE. All that we know about God and Jesus, we learn from the Bible. I believe that the Bible is the authoritative document of our faith. Today we have some who are living two or more millenniums after the events recorded in the Bible — yet they believe that they have a better understanding of what happened than those who were eye witnesses. In all matters of faith and life, the Scriptures speak with divine authority.

I BELIEVE IN FORGIVENESS. Of all the doctrines of the Christian faith, none is more important than the doctrine of forgiveness. Forgiveness begins with our receiving divine forgiveness and ends with our giving human forgiveness. It is as we pray, 'Forgive us our debts, as we forgive our debtors.' We are all sinners. The only way that sinners can live together is by learning to forgive each other.

I BELIEVE IN THE CHURCH. The church is at its best when it is the family of God.

> We share each other's woes,
> Each other's burdens bear,
> And often for each other flows
> The sympathizing tear.

The church is also the custodian and guardian of the faith. It is the duty of the church to see that the Scriptures are correctly interpreted. A private opinion is to be rejected if it is contrary to the teaching of the church as a whole.

I BELIEVE IN THE RESURRECTION. If there is any

one doctrine which is distinctive of the Christian faith, it is the doctrine of the resurrection and the life everlasting. Paul insisted that if Jesus did not rise from the dead, the Christian faith was a fraud. As surely as there is Easter, we have the assurance that death is not the end but a new beginning. Alfred Tennyson wrote:

Thou wilt not leave us in the dust:
Thou madest man, he knows not why.
He thinks he was not made to die;
And Thou hast made him: Thou art just.

I BELIEVE IN THE KINGDOM OF GOD. God will bring an end to history. Humankind will not continue on this planet until the sun fades and the earth grows cold. One day the kingdoms of this world will become the kingdoms of our Lord and of his Christ: and He shall reign for ever and ever. (Revelation 11:15 King James Version.) When that final day will come, we do not know. But we are assured that it will come."

Tom retired October 31, 1995 and credits Ruth with being more than his helpmate through all the years of their marriage:

"Very few men will be successful without the support and encouragement of their wives. From the beginning of our marriage in May of 1947, Ruth has actively worked with me in all areas of our ministry. Although many men have supportive wives, Ruth has the academic background and theological degree to be a full partner.

In life we often walk in green pastures and drink from the still waters. Life also takes us through the valley of shadows. Ministers, in a special way, both suffer and rejoice with their congregations. They suffer as they perform the funerals of friends, and they rejoice in the baptisms and weddings. Having ministered to four congregations, Ruth and I have sought to be the means by which God has blessed others on their way."

A new minister was sought. He would be wise to read Dr. Kirkman's sermon, delivered March 7, 1993 entitled:

LANDMARKS

Text: "Remove not the ancient landmarks which thy fathers have set."
(Proverbs 22:28 King James Version)

The commandment to preserve the ancient landmarks
is found four times in the Old Testament:
(Deut. 19:14, 27:17; Proverbs 22:28, 23:10)

The Hebrews were commanded to remember the events
that had shaped their history.
They remembered the giving of the law to Moses,
David's victory over the giant, Goliath,
And Elijah's triumph over the priests of Baal.
The Hebrews remembered where these events
had occurred.

In remembering their history, they understood their identity as a people.
They were reminded of God's providence over their nation.

With our restoration and expansion program,
The Royal Poinciana Chapel has prepared itself for ministry
in the coming new century.
We also have landmarks which define our history and our identity.
The person who most shaped this Chapel
was Henry Morrison Flagler.

For many of us whose roots are not in Florida,
it is difficult to appreciate the towering stature of Mr. Flagler.
One story (which my source affirms to be true) gives you
some idea of the high esteem in which Flagler was held.

Mr. Flagler was a friend of Thomas Edison and Henry Ford.
>One day the three men were out riding in a car
>>and got stuck in the sand.
>>>A farmer with his team of horses pulled the car out.
>>>>Mr. Flagler introduced himself and his friends to the farmer,

'I'm Henry Flagler; this is Thomas Edison; and that is Henry Ford.
>Who are you?'
>>The farmer looked at the three men in disbelief and replied,
>>>'I guess that in this crowd the only person left to be
>>>>is Jesus Christ!'

Flagler, who originally gave the money for the building of this Chapel,
>expressed his hope and ambition for the Chapel.
>>He saw the Chapel as a unique expression of the Christian faith.
>>>I believe that four of Flagler's principles
>>>>should help us to set our course for the coming century.

I. THE CHAPEL SHOULD BE NONDENOMINATIONAL.
First, Mr. Flagler believed
>that the Chapel should always be nondenominational.
>>He did not want the Chapel to be the captive
>>>of any religious organization.
>This may be a reflection of his independent spirit,
>>but the wave of the future has proved his good judgment.
>>>Today all of the major denominations are in decline,
>>>>and the independent churches are, in the main, growing.

Some years ago, a reporter from *The Atlanta Constitution* called
>to get some information about the Chapel.
He asked, 'What denomination is the Chapel?'
>'None,' I replied.
'Don't you have a bishop or superintendent to whom you report?'
>'No, we cut the middle men out
>>and report directly to God,' I said.

I am sure that Henry Flagler wanted it that way.
    We do not answer to any ecclesiastical bureaucracy.

II. THE CHAPEL SHOULD BE INTERDENOMINATIONAL.
Although Mr. Flagler did not use the word,
    he also wanted the Chapel to be interdenominational.
        He wanted winter visitors to Palm Beach
            to worship together
                and experience the unity of the Christian faith.

Several years ago, the Chapel made a survey
    of the different denominations represented in our congregation.
        It may surprise you to know
            that at least 21 different denominational affiliations
                were represented in our congregation.
    In my judgment, this is as it should be.
        The first allegiance of every Christian is to Jesus Christ.

It is reported that John Wesley, founder of the Methodist Church,
    had a dream that he had just entered heaven.
        He asked his guide to take him where the Methodists were.

The guide said, 'We have no Methodists here.
    We have only those who have washed themselves
        in the blood of the Lamb,
    and of them we have a great multitude that no man can number
        from every kindred, tongue, and race.'
    God does not see us as members of a denomination
        He sees us as believers in Jesus Christ.

III. THE CHAPEL SHOULD HAVE THE FREEST PULPIT.
Third, Flagler wanted the Chapel to be the freest pulpit in the world.
    He did not want the pastor of the Chapel
        to be bound by the prejudices of a congregation.
            The minister should preach his conscience.

Another Chapel story concerns Dr. George Morgan Ward.
Dr. Ward preached a sermon which was considered controversial.
After the service, two men walked out of the Chapel together.
One said to the other,
'If that preacher continues to preach like that,
he won't last long in Palm Beach!'

The other man took a different point of view.
He said, 'I disagree.
Dr. Ward has a great many friends in town,
and I am one of them.
My name is Henry Flagler.'

For the record, Dr. Ward served as the pastor of the Chapel
for thirty years.

IV. THE CHAPEL SHOULD BE DEBT FREE.
Finally, Henry Flagler believed that the Chapel should be debt free.
As a successful businessman,
he understood the need to operate without debt.

In the early days the Chapel was open for worship
only three months of the year.
The year round expenses of the Chapel had to be supported
by those who were here only for the winter.
With the advent of air conditioning,
the Chapel was open for a longer period.
It has been only a little over a decade
that the Chapel has been open year round.

The Chapel had no difficulty in being debt free in Flagler's day.
For a time, Mr. Flagler owned the Chapel,
and the church was largely supported by him.
Even after his death, the Chapel's physical facilities
were maintained by the Flagler system.

I am happy to report that today the Chapel is debt free.

The improvements made in the interior of the Chapel four years ago
were subscribed before the work began.

The almost two million dollars needed to remanufacture the organ,
restore the exterior of the Chapel,
and furnish our new building has been subscribed.
The total amount pledged will cover the cost of this work.

I believe that the Chapel has been faithful
to the standards Mr. Flagler set for us.
I hope that the Chapel will always be free and independent
never falling under the control of a denomination.
I hope that the Chapel will always be open to all Christians.
Our membership should reflect the diversity
of the Christian faith.

I support the view that the Chapel's pulpit should be free.
I probably would not last long as your pastor if it were otherwise.
The Chapel should always be supported by its members,
and those who worship here should keep it free from debt.

A picture of Henry Morrison Flagler hangs in the foyer of the new building.
May his hopes for this Chapel guide its future."

Another transition, another era beginning. Constant change but still the memories of those who author this history. Louise Gillett worked for eighteen years at her "temporary" post alongside daughter Marilyn, as "Financial Secretary." Louise worked with Dr. Lindsay and with Dr. Miller and with Dr. Kirkman and Ruth. She was particularly flattered at her retirement when she was presented with a check and given a standing ovation by the Chapel members at the Annual Meeting. "I felt privileged to work with so many highly educated people and I have always loved the Chapel ... I've made so many wonderful friends there."

Marilyn Polete relates well to those emotions expressed by Louise. Her memories of Dr. Lindsay richly enhanced her life work and the continuum of ministers since the Lindsay era are vividly etched. She worked for the Chapel for thirty years and chose to retire when Dr. Kirkman retired. Her devotion to the Chapel cannot be overstated. While Marilyn is no longer listed in the bulletin as "Secretary" she rarely misses a Sunday service as husband Richard performs the duty of usher each week. Marilyn's role has been significant and she continues to be a part of the ongoing life of the Chapel, witnessing with keen interest the various transitions through the years of the Little White Church by the Trail.

$\mathcal{D}$R. RICHARD MARLIN CROMIE

Dr. Kirkman knew John C. ("Skip") Randolph from Royal Oak. Raised in Huntington Woods, an adjoining suburb, Skip was one of many students whom Tom took through catechism and also baptized. When Skip's father became ill, they moved to Florida. When Tom received the call from the Chapel, Skip was Chairman of the Pulpit Committee for Lakeside Presbyterian Church and asked Tom why he wouldn't consider becoming minister at the Presbyterian Church. Tom answered, "If I wanted that kind of church, I would have stayed in Royal Oak."

Skip, at one time, thought he might go to seminary but went to law school instead and ultimately became Palm Beach Town Attorney. He left Lakeside to join the Chapel where he occasionally filled the pulpit to sermonize "when Dr. Kirkman was out of town."

Skip was President of the Board of Directors when Tom announced his retirement. A Search Committee was formed with Chester Claudon as Chairman. George Slaton was Vice-Chairman.

It took two telephone calls before Dr. Cromie sent his résumé or dossier to the Chapel. When Dr. Kirkman called the first time Dr. Cromie was totally surprised, "Tom Kirkman called and said that some of the Chapel people, with Don Carmichael leading the way, were coming down (to Fort Lauderdale) to hear me preach. He asked that I send my résumé. I informed Dr. Kirkman that it was not up to date. It was in June of '95 when Tom called again, from North Carolina and said, 'Richard, you're foolish not to consider the Chapel ... they are wonderful people ... you should at least take a look.'"

Margaret Waddell was asked to serve on the Search Committee. Raised a Methodist, Margaret joined the Chapel in 1989 and her long-term membership and active participation as member of the administrative board and also as trustee in the Methodist Church were valuable credentials. According to Dr. Cromie, "Marshall McDonald flew down from North Carolina and Chester Claudon came from Michigan to check me out. A group of us had lunch at the Lauderdale Yacht Club on that occasion. When Peggy and I were invited to Palm Beach to dinner at the Carmichaels, there were about twenty people in attendance. In their words they felt that 'God led us to call you.' I answered, let me pray about it and talk to Peggy ... I can't really answer exactly why I accepted the call ... it was just something in my heart. The opportunity came at a time when we had been looking ... everything we'd set out to accomplish in Fort Lauderdale had been achieved. I'm a restless kind of person with a great deal of God-given energy. I'd taken a look at the Presidency of a Seminary and at a large church up north but we decided against both. But I had an inkling, similar to how I felt while at Southminster, where everything was just fine ... but I felt a stirring then in my heart and it is at that time when I know that a different direction, a different path is before us."

"Quite honestly", Dr. Cromie concedes, "Palm Beach represented a relief. The membership in Fort Lauderdale had grown from 2180 to 3100, with a staff of seventy-two, including a Retirement Home, a Pre-school and a massive church. I was moving on to a staff of three. Hopefully I would gain the opportunity to write and publish more books, but that hope did not materialize entirely. I have managed to publish two books since coming to the Chapel. I tend to become involved in everything and in Palm Beach I soon found many new challenges not only within the Chapel but in the community."

The new minister's path had taken him from a childhood in Pittsburgh through graduation from the University of Pittsburgh in 1957 and then to Pittsburgh Theological Seminary, graduating with honors in 1962. He was a Rotary Foundation Fellow in 1958-59 at the University of St. Andrews where he exercized his love of golf which began at age ten when he won a caddy tournament. He played often on the fabled Scottish links within the shadow of the Royal and Ancient Clubhouse of St. Andrews. He had been on the staff of the Shadyside Presbyterian Church in Pittsburgh and Pastor at Parkwood Church in Allison Park, as well as College Pastor at Carnegie-Mellon University. He was Senior Pastor at the Southminster Presbyterian Church in Mount Lebanon, Pennsylvania from 1973 to 1983 and it is there where Hank McCall's mother, Florence Gill McCall, "dragged me to hear Dr. Cromie ... mother just exalted him ..." According to Hank the accolades were impressive from the Renaissance woman, a Phi Beta Kappa at the University of Texas who gained her masters degree in geology. Her approbation was particularly significant in light of raising three children in Mount Lebanon where she established a reputation for brilliance as a book reviewer and proffering educated criticism in many quarters. "She was impossibly critical of her daughters-in-law and I made a determination that wherever Irmie and I settled, there always be at least a thousand miles separating us from Mount Lebanon." Hank remembers, "Dr. Cromie was an enthusiastic young minister, having studied in Scotland, and mother, who lived to be ninety- six, made certain that her seat every Sunday

DEBBIE SCHATZ, PALM BEACH DAILY NEWS

Christmas Boutique Top: Ann and Donald Carmichael with Dr. Cromie. Bottom left to right: Ken Richter, Ted Hepburn and Dick Harrington

morning was close to the front of the sanctuary to better hear her favorite minister."

Richard Cromie married Margaret (Peggy) Good on September 2, 1959. Peggy, not from a ministerial family, was led to believe by Richard that she was marrying a future Professor of Theology, not a parish minister. The marriage was blessed with three daughters, Catherine Alice, Anne Campbell "Cammie" and Courtney Beth. The two older girls were in college when the Cromies left Mt. Lebanon for Ft. Lauderdale.

Before accepting the Chapel's call Dr. Cromie had been Senior Pastor of the First Presbyterian Church in Fort Lauderdale for twelve years. He is candid in his appraisal of what he found when he came south. "When I took over there were many areas of need. The whole complex was run-down and there was no endowment to speak of. We set out on a five-year plan which became a ten-year plan to update the properties. New air conditioning was needed in the sanctuary and in the Christian Education building. There was no suitable place for what was called the Pink House Art Ministry. My predecessor, Dr. Clem Bininger, had worked out of his home like many of the ministers of his generation. We built a new office complex and a new Christian Education building. We refurbished the sanctuary and bought an office building on Las Olas Boulevard for the Pink House Ministry and performed extensive remodeling of Westminster Manor Retirement Home. Near-by houses were bought and torn down to provide additional church parking."

"Our goals were to develop," according to Dr. Cromie, "programs for people of all ages. We started the Adult Activities Center where three hundred people participated, patterned after a similar program in Mt. Lebanon. I gave book reviews once a month and there were weekly educational and recreational programs that kept the church dynamically involved in the lives of many members and visitors. We also gave forty scholarships every year to college students. I believe firmly that if you give someone a good education, a good self-image, you contribute substantially to the betterment of society as a whole. We were also actively involved in Habitat for Humanity, building two houses a year. The most gratifying outreach program was the building of a Burn Unit in the Louis Aybar Hospital in Santo Domingo. We made several trips to the Caribbean Island in what was our most ambitious mission, initiated by Lewis J. Ort who persuaded me and then the church that we could handle the four million dollar commitment. Courtney, our youngest daughter, accompanied us, along with some members of the congregation, to Santo Domingo for the dedication of the hospital and it was a wonderful experience for all of us. It was a particularly vivid revelation to Courtney of what the ministry, through faith, can achieve. I'm certain it was a defining pilgrimage determining her chosen course of study toward a career."

Dr. Cromie's past ministerial experience involved him in the work of the Presbyterian Church, having served as Moderator of Pittsburgh Presbytery, and as Committee Chairman of the General Assembly. He also served on the Board of Trustees of the Center of Theological Inquiry in Princeton, and serves on the Board at Columbia Theological Seminary in Decatur, Georgia. He has always been active in community endeavors. Soon after accepting the call

Habitat House, Boynton Beach (1997)

in Palm Beach he became a board member of the Palm Beach Fellowship of Christians and Jews, The United Way of the Palm Beaches, and Growing Together, a drug rehabilitation center for young people.

Anne Carmichael, as a member of the Benevolence Committee, had begun seeking students for scholarship funding while Dr. Kirkman was still minister. However, according to Anne, "We did not go full-fledged with a scholarship fund until Dr. Cromie became our minister. It was within his ministry that the inception of a major scholarship program was initiated." Anne shares, from the minutes of a Benevolence Committee meeting, the philosophy guiding the committee: 'Since we are a Christian Chapel we attempt to identify and support Christian efforts. There are three facets that we hope to reach through giving: Social Outreach, local organizations and the mission beyond.' The report explained how the different organizations that were listed fall into each category. "The scholarships are given in a two-prong effort: one is that the giving will go to minorities and the second phase will honor and aid youngsters from the Chapel family and friends. While the greatest need is in the minority sector, we feel it is important to recognize that the committee is working hard to develop both phases."

Anne continues, "Ten years ago, early in the Kirkman ministry, the benevolent committee was giving away about ten thousand dollars each year and that was the amount for some years. When the benevolence budget of the Chapel increased to twenty thousand, with the boutique and other funding included, the benevolent total increased our benevolences to fifty-four thousand dollars. For 1997 we are budgeting approximately eighty-two thousand. The Habitat house falls within the Outreach Program and we are committed to funding thirty-thousand dollars toward the house in Lantana. There have been between fifty to sixty volunteers from the Chapel actively engaged in building and painting the house."

"Focusing on children," Anne explains, "we were involved with the Boy Scout program for underprivileged as well as the Boys and Girls Clubs in Belle Glade and The Rehabilitation Center for Children and Adults in Palm Beach. Reaching out to various Christian organizations we have sent funds to the Salvation Army, The Gideons, Campus Crusade for Christ, a jail ministry program, a building fund for a Presbyterian Church west of the city as well as funding for churches that were burned by arsonists. We also established a Chapel emergency relief fund for hurricane and floods and sent money to a church in Wilmington which had experienced damage from a hurricane. We work with the migrants of Florida and are expanding our scholarship programs. We are always looking for areas of need and when they come to our attention, we try to address them."

"The dinner auction begun in 1996 will be chaired in 1998 by Sam and Joyce McClendon in an ongoing effort to keep increasing our income for benevolences because the needs are so great ..." Anne gives special praise to Dr. Cromie, "He's a dream to work with, is focused and I think his message is always poignant."

It was a little over a year of Dr. Cromie's pastorate at the Chapel when he presided over the first Scottish Reformation Sunday service January 26, 1997. He had pioneered Scottish services in Pittsburgh and Ft. Lauderdale. The publicity of the pending service portraying the portly minister wearing his kilt drew a packed house. The hymn "Amazing Grace" was accompanied by Pipes and Organ and the sermon "Heave Awa' Lads, We're Nae Deid Yet!" was accompanied by reference: "Therefore take the whole armor of God ... and having done all, to stand!" Ephesians 6:13.

The bulletin further explained the significance of the special service:

> "CEUD MILE FAILTE ...
>
> 'One Hundred Thousand Welcomes' greet you this morning as we tip our tartans to the Scottish origin of the Reformed Church. Our Chapel is interdenominational, and selects no particular denominational origin for special honor. But, Mr. Henry Flagler's father was a Presbyterian Pastor. Henry Flagler, who built this Chapel, also built the St. Augustine Memorial Presbyterian Church, in memory of his daughter, Jennie. Within that church is a mausoleum where Jennie and her parents are buried.
>
> While he was a Presbyterian, Mr. Flagler's church interests were not limited to that denomination. He was extremely generous to churches of all denominations in the Palm Beach area and far, far beyond.
>
> CEUD MILE TAING!
>
> To those leading the Worship and the Celebration:
>
> Rob Latimer, Piper

Dr. Cromie with Courtney Beth

Ft. Lauderdale Pipe and Drum Corps
Chauncey Grey, Drummer
Malcolm Arnold, Soloist
Lachlan Reed, Lay Reader
Hazel Kennedy, Supervisor of Reception
Thanks to all who helped."
As the Chapel history continues to evolve, the minister, the board, and church members, and all the people involved are its authors. 'Dr. Cromie', his dossier reads, 'as member of the American Society of Literary Scholars, has published, SOMETIME BEFORE THE DAWN, HOW TO LIVE WITH CANCER, CHRIST WILL SEE YOU THROUGH, THE FUTURE IS NOW, WHEN YOU LOSE SOMEONE

Wednesday Morning Bible Class
Madge Yoakley on left and Suzanne Slaton at piano

YOU LOVE, and THE RHAPSODY OF SCRIPTURE. As President of Desert Ministries, Inc., he is actively engaged in producing books and pamphlets for use of clergy and laity as well as sponsoring broadcasts of his sermons. He also speaks at conventions and conferences including the Chautauqua Institution in New York and the Conference Grounds in Ocean Park, Maine.'

The bulletin for February 16, 1997 includes an insert presenting a luncheon in Celebration of Biblical Women in addition to a notice announcing: "Habitat for Humanity is here ... In the next few weeks we will begin to build our Habitat for Humanity House. Volunteers are needed." There was also the announced Piano-Organ Concert to be presented by Barbara Pearson Johnson and Dr. Jack Jones, including the works by Schubert, Massenet, Boud, Nielson-Young and unusual hymn arrangements combined with the classical melodies of Mozart, Beethoven and Rachmaninoff.

Also a THANK YOU was included. "The Reverend Courtney B. Cromie and her family would like to thank all of you who, in so many different ways, added to the joy of the Ordination last

Sunday." The Reverend Courtney B. Cromie now serves at Colesville Presbyterian Church in Silver Spring, Maryland as Associate Pastor.

There was also the regularly announced 'Wednesday Morning Bible Study.' For the past twenty years, in a continuance dating from the Lindsay era, its inclusion in the bulletin read: 'Madge Yoakley's Bible Study Group meets every Wednesday at 10:30 a.m. All are welcome.'

In another testimony to Henry Flagler's legacy, the Chapel continues to welcome non-members and those who provide spiritual outreach. Madge explains how it came to be that she has served the Chapel. Her husband, attorney David S. Yoakley, "was a great friend of Dr. Lindsay. One morning as they were enjoying coffee at Green's (Pharmacy), David told Dr. Lindsay about my three-year-old Bible class, attracting thirty to forty ladies from various churches to studies held in their homes. Dr. Lindsay was enthusiastic about the study and invited me to use the Small Chapel for the meetings. From that time on, from October through May, there has been a gathering of Episcopalians, Presbyterians, Catholics, Chapel members and Jewish ladies attending the weekly sessions. Suzanne Slaton always arrived early to play the piano to set a joyful tone for the meeting. After the opening hymn, prayer and a recitation of the books of the Bible, Genesis to Revelation, the lesson is given." Madge is keen to relay her motto, "Teaching but no preaching ... and it's very hard to keep from straying over the line. The theme always begins with a subject in Ephesians and from there it jumps to any chapter in the Bible. My routine has been to perform all the preparation, planning the matrix, the basic skeleton of the lectures, during the summer months, and then when October arrives I plan the weekly sessions as they present themselves. I am not a trained theologian or Bible student, but have always depended on the Lord for guidance. This truly has been a labor of love, always with the main objective to find joy and fun and to have a pleasant time learning the Scriptures."

Apparently from Madge's view, "during declining years the

small gathering was a significant source and spark of life for the Chapel." Obviously, the blessings to the Little White Church by the Trail continue bountifully.

The year round church with a new minister in the pulpit would feel energized. There were new members and some old members would find it difficult to accept the transition from the beloved Tom Kirkman to the "new man." However, the history continued. On February 21, 1997: IN MEMORIAM, MURIEL VEDDER (Mrs. Matthew) CATUNA. And a notice of the Chapel Chorus which was an innovation: "The ever-popular Royal Poinciana Chapel Chorus will resume rehearsals today. The chorus will be preparing three exciting anthems to sing on Palm Sunday. All Chapel members and friends are invited to participate."

The March 9th bulletin held the announced passing of Carl H. Eiser, February 28, 1997, an usher for forty years, as another thread in the Chapel history became secure in the life ever-lasting. The same bulletin held the listing of the Board of Directors:

> Chester Claudon, President
> George C. Slaton, Vice President
> Judy Golembiewski, Treasurer
> James ("Buck") Alban, Jr.
> Donald Carmichael
> John C. ("Skip) Randolph
> Marshall McDonald (At Large)

On Sunday, the sixteenth of March, Dr. Cromie's sermon was "Life Is What Happens When...", the Text: "Again I saw that the race is not to the swift, or the battle to the strong ... but time and chance happen to them all." Ecclesiastes 9:11.

Some excerpts indicate the style and substance attributed to the new minister:

> "I always have the feeling that something important is going on when I get to the book of Ecclesiastes. Koheleth, the author, has long been a 'friend' of mine. He is honest. I like the man who tells me what he knows: 'I have tried everything under the sun, and I

have found that all of it is vanity.' Life is tough. 'All you have to do,' he says, 'is to fear God and keep God's Commandments ... But meanwhile, don't expect too much.'

Ecclesiastes is deep. Much of the Bible is told in simple little stories, which even a child can understand. They are not that simple, but you can lock into them at any level. With Ecclesiastes you have to stretch.

'I wish I could tell you (Koheleth speaking) that everything will end happily. But, frankly, I am not always too sure of that.' Once in a while you have to walk out on the edge ... what Paul Tillich called 'The Boundary.' If you can stare into the abyss at the heart of things and come back smiling, you can appreciate the message of Koheleth.

In Chapter Nine he writes: 'Enjoy life all the days of your life. Whatever you find do, do it with all your might; for there is no work, or thought, or knowledge, or wisdom in Shoel, where you are going.' In other words, you only go around once, give and get all the gusto you can ... beyond that, who knows? 'I saw under the sun that the race is not to the swift, nor is the battle to the strong, but time and chance happen to them all.'

Time and chance happen to them all. They do. The rain falls on the just and the unjust. Good people suffer, just like the others ... A friend of mine in trouble, went up to Rochester to the Mayo Clinic. He asked, 'Why did this happen to me?' The doctor said, 'I don't know ... I guess it's just your turn.'

Is it fair? Of course not! Some people seem to have far more than their share ... their turn seems to come up far too frequently. Is God up to some kind of trick? No ... but keep listening. One day at Muirfield at the British Open, the rough was so high, a couple of caddies got lost. The reporter asked Jack Nicklaus if he thought the course was fair. He said, 'I didn't think golf was intended to be fair. It's intended to be a challenge!'

Hugh Thomson Kerr, Jr., in his lead editorial in Theology Today told of how he was planning to go to a conference in Tucson. Some difficult things happened to his family on the way. They ended up in the emergency room. They had to be flown back to New Jersey. They hired a driver to bring their car, but he got into an accident and totaled the car.

Dr. Kerr wrote: 'Isn't it peculiar that I, who all my life had preached to people about trusting in the Will of God, was struggling with why He had chosen me for all this.' His faith began to falter. One trusty classmate advised: 'Don't worry about it, Tim, life is what happens when ... you are planning something else!'

When I was a boy in the early 1940s, the young men and women who were leaving school, then as now, were planning to go off to college, or to start work in the family business, ... Then December 7, 1941 came along, and their lives were changed forever. Life is what happened to them and their loved ones as they were planning something else ... and it was three, four, five years before they returned, and ... some of them never came back at all.

We all know those who have faced illness, or uncertainty, or goodness knows what. Sometimes it was an accident on the highway. Sometimes a divorce ... sometimes family violence, sometimes alcohol ... life is what happens when you are planning something else. And, the very frailties of the human body catch up to you, like one of my Fort Lauderdale friends says, 'My longevity is catching up to me!'

Peter, Andrew, James, and John were fishermen on the Galilean Sea. I have been there: beautiful lake, quiet little towns, lots of open country. People are nicer there, and you can leave your doors open ... They loved the water and their seaside town, time to talk, time to loaf ... But, one day, as they were mending their nets, along came Jesus Christ. Without warning, He said, 'Come and follow me.'

'Where?'

'Wherever, just come ... I will make you fishers of men. Your days on the lake are over. You will face abuse and rejection, but in the end, it will be worth it.'

By the way ... have you, here at the Chapel, ever sacrificed anything for Christ? Has your faith ever cost you anything great? Not in money so much as in time and energy. Have you really surrendered yourself and everything you have to the Lord? In the end it will be worth it.

... Our Lord ... who ever had more right to a perfect, happy life than He? And what happened? He was home in Nazareth, taking care of his mother, and God said: 'Time's up. We are leaving here.'

'To where, Lord?'

'Just come. I will show you. They will be mean to you, you will suffer abuse and be rejected ... for my sake. In the end they will hang you on a cross.'

He wandered in the wilderness in the towns and cities, until it was time for Calvary: 'Why Lord? Why me?'

'Someday I will explain it to you, just say it's our turn.' Life is what happens when God makes other plans.

My professor of preaching said to his student 35 years ago, 'Now that you have lavishly laid out the problem what do you want us to do about it?'

1. We have to realize that it is intended to be this way: time and chance happen to us all. Life is not laid out on a computerized map, which takes us directly

Sunday School (1997) Clockwise: Teacher Debra Crandall, Chad Crandall, Jessica and Cristina Clarke, Sara Edwards, Chelsea Ross, Eric Feng and Christian Crandall.

from one point to another. What was true with our Lord is also true with us: at each intersection ... we need to pause in thought and prayer, to say, 'Lord, show me the way to go next.'

2. We need to keep on going anyway. If life is not worth living, what else are you going to do with it: What is hidden now will one day be made known. In AA they sometimes say, 'Fake it 'til you make it.' Keep believing, and it will soon come true.

3. You need to be sure that you are following the one who knows the way. We lived for a couple of years in the ancient Kingdom of Fife in Scotland. Little painted road signs were usually at the crossroads to tell you which way to go, say to Anstruther, or Dundee, or Kingsbarns ... once in a while however, the mischievous young boys of Fife would play a trick and turn the signs around. But in my car one day was a local who knew the way. 'No matter what it says,' he said, 'turn north to go to Dundee.' He knew the way. I pray God you and I will learn to follow. Christ knows the way."

"Life is what happens when ..." Life will continue to happen in the "Little White Church by the Trail." The bulletin for July 20, 1997, confirms and gives witness to the high quality musical accompaniment that has always enhanced the Chapel. Those attending the mid-July worship service were gifted with the music of the world renowned Budapest Chamber String Quartet. The four young musicians, violinists Katalin Prohle and Terez Korondi, Csaba Galfi playing the viola and cellist Marcell Vamos, performed Beethoven's Piano Quartet Op. 152 No. 3 in C Major as the Prelude, with Renée LaBonté at the piano. The quartet also performed in Kirkman Hall following the service, emitting wondrous strains of Beethoven, Weiner and Heinrich in a musical celebration that perfectly epitomizes the fulfillment of Henry Flagler's musical legacy.

Dr. Cromie was in the pulpit on Sunday, July 27th. He announced that he and Peggy planned to leave that afternoon for a holiday in Ireland. The service was unique in many respects. Cindy Dedo, Soprano, performed 'Softly and Tenderly' accompanied by her own signing which Dr. Cromie drew attention to by requesting that Cindy teach the congregants to sign 'God Loves You' and 'I Love God.' Following the signing lesson, mimicked by most everyone in attendance, Nikolas Green, one of a dozen recipients of Chapel scholarship funding, read the Scripture Lesson.

A notice in the bulletin announced: 'Cassette Ministry ... Dr. Cromie and the Board are looking into whether we should begin a cassette tape ministry for our shut-ins and friends far away. We will have to purchase the necessary equipment and have a person make the tapes. It might be a good way to share the music and worship of our Chapel.'

During the service Anne Carmichael, as Chairman of the Benevolence Committee, introduced the Chapel Scholars First Year Recipients:

Chemeka L. Bannister - Palm Beach Community College
Nikolas S. Green - University of Notre Dame
Adrian A. Hill - Palm Beach Community College
Sharnette S. Pettigrew - Palm Beach Community College

Shelbie R. Rankin - Palm Beach Community College

E. Warren Twiggs - Clark Atlanta University

and the Second Year Recipients were called forward:

Kristi J. Lowery - Florida A & M University

Erin D. Mosley - Palm Beach Community College

Timothy L. Shannon - Fisk University

Shawn L. Stinson - Bethune-Cookman College

Ralph Reynolds - Palm Beach Community College

The students performed a Gospel hymn and the parishioners were encouraged to clap hands in a lively and extraordinary Sunday service in the Chapel that Henry Flagler built. The signing for the deaf, an outreach program initiated to tape future services, scholarship monies allocated and the rousing sounds of soul music and attendant clapping all eloquently exemplified Flagler's behests in a true spirit of Ecumenism.

With the richness of so many blessings within the simple white Chapel, let us hope and pray that from this day forward the peace and love of the Lord continues to magnify as Dr. Richard Cromie presides in the pulpit and as others come to serve and enrich the lives of those who gather within its hallowed walls - walls that have stood firmly for a hundred years - walls that hold the very essence of Henry Morrison Flagler as the message and the music that gave solace years before, continues to echo through the ancient sanctuary.

1898 - 1998

$\mathscr{A}$N ODE TO
THE FUTURE

GREER GATUSO

Ali Ross

To thee, White Temple by the Trail
Where Jesus sets the guiding sail;
We worship here our lovely Lord
By each and everyone adored.
May song be sung and truth be said
For another fifty years ahead;
When we have gone to be with God
From this dear place our feet have trod.

—Dr. Newton E. Davis
March 13, 1949